Instructor's Manual
with Tests

Adult Development and Aging
Myths and Emerging Realities

Third Edition

Richard Schulz

Timothy Salthouse

PRENTICE HALL, Upper Saddle River, New Jersey 07458

© 1999 by PRENTICE-HALL, INC.
Upper Saddle River, New Jersey 07458

All rights reserved

10 9 8 7 6 5 4 3 2 1

ISBN 0-13-082733-9

Printed in the United States of America

INTRODUCTION

All of us hold strong beliefs about what it means to be an adult, and what it means to grow old. Some of these beliefs are positive-focusing on the vitality, productivity, rights and privileges of adulthood. Other beliefs may be negative-dwelling on images of declining health, restricted freedom, loneliness and, ultimately, death. Each individual's constellation of beliefs is unique, shaped by family history, interactions with relatives and friends, and a multitude of life experiences. Often these beliefs are assumed to be "givens" or facts of adulthood and aging. In reality, at least some of these deeply held beliefs may be myths based on limited and biased information. As individuals become serious students of adult development and aging, they have a responsibility to examine their beliefs in the light of scientific evidence. The textbook, Adult Development and Aging, is written to facilitate this process of thoughtful examination. Research findings on ten dimensions of adult development and aging are systematically analyzed in Chapters 3 - 12, and commonly held myths are contrasted with the best available scientific evidence. In addition, the authors explain the strengths and limitations of various research methods used to study issues of adult development and aging. By understanding these research methods, students will be better prepared to continue a critical examination of newly published research findings.

Unfortunately, the presentation of scientific evidence is not always suffi-cient to change cherished beliefs. Often students need an opportunity to relate theoretical information to their personal experiences before they can begin to recognize their assumptions, question the validity of those assump-tions, assimilate new information, and modify their beliefs. The purpose of this Instructor's Manual is to complement the scientific thrust of the textbook and to suggest ways in which students can be helped to integrate theoretical information into their personal frame of reference.

The authors hope that this manual will prove useful to instructors as they plan courses, develop lectures, and design lessons. Instructors are invited to select the material that fits most comfortably with their own style of teaching as well as with the level of student enrolled in a given course. For example, instructors who prefer to lecture and who teach undergraduate students could prepare a series of lecture outlines following the content of each textbook chapter. The text could then be used to reinforce the presentation of information and for student review. The objective test questions provided in this manual could be used to assess the degree to which students comprehend the information being presented. Alternatively, instructors who value more experiential modes of learning could rely on assigned textbook readings to convey facts, key concepts, and important issues. Class time could then be devoted to discussion and/or activities aimed at helping students to understand issues, examine attitudes and values, or begin to explore the practical applications of the information. Regardless of how an instructor decides to use the textbook and the material in this manual, modifications that make suggested questions/activities fit more effectively into an overall instructional plan are encouraged.

The remainder of this manual is divided into twelve sections, one for each chapter of the textbook. Each section, in turn, contains objectives, discussion questions, learning activities, additional readings, and test questions. Each of these components is described more fully below.

CHAPTER OBJECTIVES

Each section of this Instructor's Manual begins with a list of learner-centered objectives, which may be shared with students. To avoid a cumbersome laundry list of detailed objectives, only the major purposes and content of each chapter are highlighted by the objectives in the Instructor's Manual. If an instructor wants to emphasize certain aspects of a chapter, however, subsidiary objectives can be written without much difficulty. For example, one purpose of the textbook is to encourage students to develop a language for studying, discussing, and thinking about adult development and aging. A major objective asks students to identify and define key concepts relevant to the content of each chapter. An instructor could expand on this objective, by writing additional objectives specifically related to terms listed in the glossary for each chapter.

Another purpose of the textbook is to encourage students to think critically about the various dimensions of adult development and aging. Objectives asking students to differentiate myths from scientific evidence or to compare and contrast various theories are included to foster analytic thinking skills. If this level of thinking is too advanced for undergraduate students, an instructor may want to rephrase the objectives by replacing analytic verbs (e.g., differentiate, compare, contrast) with more basic knowledge oriented verbs (e.g., identify, describe, label, list, match, select, state).

2

DISCUSSION QUESTIONS

The second item included in each section of the Instructor's Manual is a set of discussion questions. The purpose of these questions is to help students relate concepts and research findings to their own experiences. By exploring the implications of theoretical information in terms of their own life experiences, students should be better able to understand and retain the main ideas presented in each chapter of the textbook. If an instructor prefers to give essay rather than objective tests, the discussion questions can also be modified for use on exams.

LEARNING ACTIVITIES

The third item in each section of the Instructor's Manual is learning activities, which have a threefold purpose. First, many of these activities are designed to encourage students to have contact and interaction with adults of various ages with the intent of fostering intergenerational understanding. Second, a number of the activities require students to reflect on their own life experiences, identify their own beliefs about adult development and aging, and to translate their personal views into a basis for inquiry. Third, the activities often ask students to gather primary data, which they can compare and contrast with the research findings reported in the text. Through this process, students can begin to practice in small ways the skills of research. Hopefully, students will learn to question their own assumptions, generate questions or tentative hypotheses to explain differences between their findings and those in the literature.

ADDITIONAL READINGS

Included as the fourth item in each section of the Instructor's Manual are recommended readings. The readings are rated according to difficulty (i.e., Introductory, Intermediate, and Advanced) so that the instructor can assign readings appropriate to the students' current level of ability.

TEST QUESTIONS

The final item in each section of the Instructor's Manual is an extensive set of objective test questions based on key concepts, principles, and issues in each chapter of the textbook. Instructors can use these questions to prepare chapter quizzes or major course examinations. The questions can also be given to students for self-assessment and review.

CHAPTER 1--INTRODUCTION

CHAPTER OBJECTIVES

The purpose of this chapter is to enable students to:

Explain the difference between intraindividual changes and interindividual differences
related to aging.

Explain the difference between "life expectancy at birth" and "maximum life span."

Explain the difference between gerontology and geriatrics.

Describe the demographic trends in aging for the United States and the rest of the world.

Identify important questions and issues in gerontology/geriatrics.

DISCUSSION QUESTIONS

Describe how the percentage of the elderly in the United States is expected to change between now and 2030. Identify factors that are contributing to this change. What are the probable societal consequences of these changes?

As the population of the United States ages, do you think there will be a positive or negative impact on the quality of life in our society? Explain your reasoning. Describe the quality of life for different age groups at different points in historical time.

What are the likely consequences of a growing elderly population in developing countries? How might this affect countries such as the United States and Canada?

How might population migration affect the age composition of a population within a country?

LEARNING ACTIVITIES

What does it mean to grow old? Spend about 15 minutes writing down any thoughts, ideas, images, impressions you have in response to this question. Keep what you have written with you throughout the course, and as we study each aspect of adult development, compare and contrast what you have written with the scientific evidence presented.

Write down five adjectives that come to mind when you think about growing old. Compare your list with those of other students in the class. How similar or different are your lists? Do your adjectives reflect a positive or negative response to aging? What factors have shaped your views of aging?

Think of someone you know who is middle age and someone who is over 65 years old. How do they handle issues of aging? Would you want to be like them--why or why not?

Scan a local newspaper and identify all articles that pertain to issues of aging. What types of issues are raised and what are the prevailing views regarding these issues?

Using library resources, pick a popular magazine and compare the types of ads they contained 20 or 30 years ago versus now. What types of products are being advertised for older persons then and now; how are older persons depicted in ads then and now?

ADDITIONAL READINGS

Introductory

U. S. Bureau of the Census. 1997. Statistical Abstract of the United States, 117th Edition (Washington, DC).

Intermediate

Martin, L. G., & Preston, S. H. (Eds.) 1994. Demography of Aging. (Washington, DC: National Academy Press).

Birren, J. E., & Birren B. A. 1990. "The Concepts, Models, and History of the Psychology of Aging. In J. E. Birren & K. W. Schaie (Eds.), Handbook of the psychology of aging, 3rd Edition. (New York: Academic Press).

5

Advanced

Suzman, R. M., Willis, D. P., & Manton, K. G. (Eds.) 1992. The Oldest Old.
(New York: Oxford University Press).

MULTIPLE CHOICE QUESTIONS

1. Which of the following was (were) mentioned in the text as the function(s) of the behavioral scientist?

    a.   To describe behavioral phenomena.
    b.   To identify the underlying causes of behavior.
    c.   To apply their findings in ways that will modify the environment for the better.
*   d.   All of the above.

2. Changes that take place within the individual across the adult life span are called

*   a.   intraindividual changes.
    b.   interindividual differences.
    c.   life expectancy.
    d.   developmental differences.

3. The extent to which changes occur at different rates among different adults is called

*   a.   interindividual differences.
    b.   intraindividual differences.
    c.   gerontological differences.
    d.   developmental differences.

4. Regarding adult development, current research evidence

*   a.   does not support the concept of universally applicable stages.
    b.   verifies the existence of universal stages.
    c.   suggests that development ceases at around age forty.
    d.   suggests that stages can be applied only to adult females.

5. Which of the following does <u>NOT</u> distinguish aging from illness and disease?

    a.   Aging is inevitable.
    b.   Illness and disease may have external causes.
    c.   Illness and disease can possibly be cured or alleviated.
*   d.   Aging requires institutionalization.

6. The term which refers to the number of years that will probably be lived by the average person born in a particular year is called

*   a.   life expectancy at birth.
    b.   life expectancy at death.
    c.   life expectancy at a specific age.
    d.   maximum life span.

7. The term which refers to the number of remaining years the average individual of a given age can expect to live at a specific time is called

*   a.   life expectancy at a specific age.
    b.   life expectancy at birth.
    c.   maximum life span.
    d.   longevity prediction.

8. The maximum life span ever recorded appears to be

    a.   95 years.
*   b.   122 years.
    c.   145 years.
    d.   160 years.

9. The trend in human life expectancy from the Prehistoric era to contemporary times appears to

*   a.   have steadily increased.
    b.   have steadily decreased.
    c.   have remained unchanged.
    d.   be characterized by mild fluctuation.

10. The primary reason for the decline in mortality rates since 1900 for American infants and children appears to be

  *   a.   improved standards of public health.
       b.   the elimination of infectious disease.
       c.   the cure for cancer.
       d.   lower birth rates.

11. Since 1940, the percentage of elderly Americans

       a.   has increased very little.
  *   b.   has increased markedly.
       c.   has decreased markedly.
       d.   has decreased slightly.

12. The highest concentrations of elderly persons are generally found in

       a.   developing countries.
       b.   countries in the southern hemisphere.
  *   c.   developed countries.
       d.   countries that consume large quantities of rice.

13. The scientific study of aging and the special problems of the aged is called

  *   a.   gerontology.
       b.   geriatrics.
       c.   physiological epidemiology.
       d.   adult anthropology.

14. The medical study of the diseases, debilities and care of aged persons is called

       a.   gerontology.
  *   b.   geriatrics.
       c.   developmental psychology.
       d.   lifespan sociology.

CHAPTER 2--RESEARCH METHODS AND ISSUES

CHAPTER OBJECTIVES

The purpose of this chapter is to enable students to:

Identify and define key concepts related to research.

Compare and contrast major research methods used to study adult development and aging in terms of:

> Assumptions
> Design
> Advantages and Disadvantages

Explain the value of understanding the research methods used to conduct studies on adult development and aging.

Identify factors that affect the internal and external validity of a study.

DISCUSSION QUESTIONS

Three important sources of variation in studies of adult development and aging are "aging," "cohort" and "time of measurement." Explain how each of these factors can affect study design. Give examples.

Explain the advantages and disadvantages of longitudinal, cross-sectional, and sequential research methods.

Given the research question, "Do people become more intelligent as they grow older?" explain the pros and cons of using the following research methods:

> Longitudinal study
> Cross sectional study
> Sequential study

What type of research method would you choose to study the question: "Are the friendship and social relationships of 60 year olds in the U.S. more or less satisfying than those of 30 year olds?" Explain the reasoning behind your choice, including the advantages and disadvantages of the method.

This chapter identified three serious threats to internal validity: confounding, selective attrition, and the effects of testing. Give an example of each and discuss why it is a threat.

Is the study of adult development and aging an "exact" science? Why or why not?

LEARNING ACTIVITIES

Find a report on the results of an aging oriented study described in the popular press. Identify what type of study it was. How valid are the conclusions reported?

Identify a medication that is currently popular with older persons. Find out what types of studies were done to gain approval for this medication.

Describe experiences you or people you know have had being part of a research study. What type of study was it? Were you randomly assigned to treatment? Did you enjoy the experience? Was the study clearly explained to you? Do you feel it was a worthwhile experience?

Generate a question about adult development and/or aging that you might be interested in studying. What research method would you use and why? What variables would you study?

ADDITIONAL READINGS

Introductory

Schaie, K. W., Campbell, R. T., Meredith, W., & Rawlings, S. C. 1988. Methodological Issues in Aging Research. (New York: Springer).

Schroots, J. J. F., & Birren, J. E. 1990. "Concepts of Time and Aging in Science." In J.E. Birren & K. W. Schaie (Eds.), Handbook of the Psychology of Aging, 3rd Edition. (New York: Academic Press).

Intermediate

Andresen, E., Totherberg, B., & Zimmer, J. G. (Eds.) 1997. Assessing the Health Status of Older Adults. (New York: Springer).

Herzog, A. R., & Rodgers, W. L. 1991. "The Use of Survey Methods in Research on Older Americans." In R. Wallace (Ed.), The Epidemiology of the Elderly. (New York: Oxford University Press).

Advanced

Collins, L. M. 1996. "Measurement of Change in Research on Aging: Old and New Issues From an Individual Growth Perspective." In J. E. Birren & K W. Schaie (Eds.), Handbook of the Psychology of Aging, Fourth Edition. (New York: Academic Press).

Lawton, M. P., & Herzog, A. R. (Eds.) 1989. Special Research Methods of Gerontology. (Amityville, New York: Baywood Publsing Co).

MULTIPLE CHOICE QUESTIONS

1. Any characteristic that can take on different values is called a

*   a.   variable.
        b.   parameter.
        c.   sample.
        d.   cohort.

2. One of the goals of any study is to produce reliable results that can be generalized to

*   a.   a larger population.
        b.   the study sample.
        c.   a cohort.
        d.   the control group.

3. The mathematical procedures which estimate population parameters based on sample characteristics are called

        a.   descriptive statistics.
*   b.   inferential statistics.
        c.   population estimates.
        d.   independent variables.

4. The type of research in which one or more independent variables are manipulated in order to determine the effects on dependent variables among randomly assigned subjects is called a(n)

*   a.   experimental design.
        b.   quasiexperimental design.
        c.   correlational design.
        d.   longitudinal design.

5. The subjects who receive the research treatment to ascertain its effects belong to the

*   a.   experimental group.
        b.   control group.
        c.   placebo group.
        d.   random group.

6. The subjects who do not receive the research treatment belong to the

*   a.   control group.
        b.   experimental group.
        c.   independent group.
        d.   dependent group.

7. Quasiexperimental designs differ from experimental designs in that they

        a.   do not have an independent variable.
*   b.   do not have randomly assigned subjects to treatments.
        c.   do not have a dependent variable.
        d.   do not utilize inferential statistics.

8. One limitation of the use of quasiexperimental designs is that

*   a.   it is harder to rule out alternative explanations for the findings.
        b.   no statement can be made about the relationship between variables.
        c.   dependent variables are often not available.
        d.   there is no independent variable.

9. The most important limitation of correlational designs is that

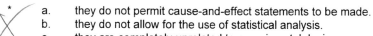

    a.   they do not permit cause-and-effect statements to be made.
    b.   they do not allow for the use of statistical analysis.
    c.   they are completely unrelated to experimental designs.
    d.   they require the designation of independent and dependent variables.

10. Which of the following is an advantage of longitudinal studies?

    a.   they provide direct information about intraindividual change.
    b.   they permit cross-cultural comparisons.
    c.   they are less expensive than cross-sectional studies.
    d.   they are resistant to the selective attrition of subjects.

11. In longitudinal studies involving difficult tasks, the amount of intraindividual change tends to be

    a.   underestimated.
    b.   overestimated.
    c.   the most accurately measured.
    d.   too difficult to measure.

12. In longitudinal studies involving simple or boring tasks, the amount of intraindividual change tends to be

    a.   underestimated.
    b.   overestimated.
    c.   the most accurately measured.
    d.   too difficult to measure.

13. Which of the following was **NOT** mentioned in the text as a difficulty with longitudinal research studies?

    a.   Psychological instruments are subject to measurement error.
    b.   Personnel turnover may result in biased interpretation of tests.
    c.   The procedures used in longitudinal studies may become outmoded.
    d.   This method confounds the influence of aging and cultures.

14. An experiment in which all measurements are performed at about the same time, usually on subjects who are of different ages is known as

*   a.   cross-sectional research.
     b.   longitudinal research.
     c.   inferential research.
     d.   dependent research.

15. Which of the following was <u>NOT</u> mentioned in the text as an advantage of cross-sectional studies?

     a.   They are less costly than longitudinal research.
     b.   The data collection process takes less time than longitudinal studies.
     c.   Research procedures are unlikely to become outmoded in the course of studies.
*   d.   They are more suitable to explain age-related differences than longitudinal studies.

16. The influence on people's behavior and personality by the social and historical forces of the generation in which they were born is called the

*   a.   cohort effect.
     b.   aging effect.
     c.   confounding effect.
     d.   sequential effect.

17. One difficulty in attempts to explain age-related differences using cross-sectional studies is

*   a.   their vulnerability to cohort effects.
     b.   their tendency to underestimate changes.
     c.   their tendency to overestimate changes.
     d.   their failure to employ the use of control groups.

18. Which of the following was <u>NOT</u> mentioned in the text as a source of variation in studies of aging and development?

     a.   aging effect.
     b.   cohort effect.
     c.   time of measurement effect.
*   d.   placebo effect.

19. An experiment which attempts to combine the longitudinal and cross-sectional methods is called

*   a.   sequential research.
       b.   mixed research.
       c.   dependent research.
       d.   strategical research.

20. A sequential research design which treats age and cohort as independent variables would be called a

*   a.   cohort-sequential strategy.
       b.   time-sequential strategy.
       c.   cross-sectional strategy.
       d.   quasi-sequential strategy.

21. A sequential research design which treats age and time of measurement as independent variables and assumes that cohort has no effect would be called

*   a.   time-sequential strategy.
       b.   cohort-sequential strategy.
       c.   cross-sectional strategy.
       d.   developmental-sequential strategy.

22. A sequential research design which treats cohort and time of measurement as independent variables and assumes that aging has no effect would be called

*   a.   cross-sectional strategy.
       b.   cohort-sequential strategy.
       c.   time-sequential strategy.
       d.   quasi-sequential strategy.

23. Which of the following would __NOT__ be considered a variation of sequential research designs?

       a.   Cohort-sequential strategy.
       b.   Time-sequential strategy.
       c.   Cross-sequential strategy.
*   d.   Multimodal-sequential strategy.

24. Which of the following was <u>NOT</u> mentioned in the text as a limitation of sequential research?

a.   Sequential designs cannot control selective attrition.
b.   It is not always possible to separate the source of variation.
c.   Sequential designs can be extremely time consuming.
*   d.   Elderly subjects often refuse to participate in sequential design studies.

25. The extent to which a study enables the researcher to identify the relationships among variables, such as cause and effect relationships, is called

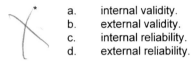

*   a.   internal validity.
b.   external validity.
c.   internal reliability.
d.   external reliability.

26. Which of the following is <u>NOT</u> a threat to a study's internal validity?

a.   Confounding.
b.   Selective attrition.
c.   Practice effect.
*   d.   Sampling procedure.

27. The extent to which research findings can be generalized from the sample to the larger population is the study's

*   a.   external validity.
b.   internal validity.
c.   external consistency.
d.   internal consistency.

28. Which of the following will affect a study's external validity?

a.   Confounding.
*   b.   Sampling procedure.
c.   Practice effect.
d.   Selective attrition.

29. The procedure in which each element of the population has an equal chance of being included in the sample is called

*   a.   random sampling.
      b.   stratified sampling.
      c.   survey sampling.
      d.   nonspecific sampling.

30. The universally accepted dividing line between middle age and old age has been found to be

      a.   age 55.
      b.   age 65.
      c.   age 72.
*   d.   different for each person.

31. If you wanted to study adults age 60 who are members of the 1930 cohort, in what year would you have to conduct your study?

      A.   1930
      B.   1960
*   C.   1990
      D.   2020

CHAPTER 3--PHYSICAL ASPECTS OF AGING

CHAPTER OBJECTIVES

The purpose of this chapter is to enable students to:

Identify and define key concepts related to physical aspects of aging.

Identify and differentiate genetic, non-genetic, and physiological theories of aging.

Identify both internally and externally visible changes associated with age.

Understand the relationship between various physiological changes and their functional consequences.

Understand the variability in the ways different individuals age.

Understand the relationship between aging and various types of illnesses.

Identify the major causes of death in the United States.

Identify factors that have been scientifically shown to contribute to longer life.

DISCUSSION QUESTIONS

When a group of adults who exercise regularly were compared with a second group of adults the same age who do not exercise at all, it was found that the first group has a significantly longer life span.

What type of research method was used in this study?
Does this study establish a cause and effect relationship between exercise and life span? Explain your answer. What variables might confound the conclusions of this study? How could you modify the design of this study to generate a more complete understanding of the relationship between exercise and life span?

If you want to live a longer life, what types of actions or behaviors might actually make a difference?

LEARNING ACTIVITIES

Examine your family's history, longevity, life style, and cause of death. Given this information, what is the prognosis for your own aging?

Try to determine at what ages professional athletes perform best at different sports. What does this tell you about physical development of human beings?

Bring to class one or two advertisements for products that are supposed to prevent or slow down physiological aging. What is the basis of the product's appeal? What scientific evidence of the product's effectiveness is provided? How would you advise someone who wants your opinion about using the product?

ADDITIONAL READINGS

Introductory

Williams, M. E. 1995. A Complete Guide to Aging and Health. (New York: Harmony).

Intermediate

Hayflick, L. 1986. "The Cell Biology of Human Aging". Scientific American: 242, 58-65.

Advanced

Miller, R. A. 1995. "Aging and the Immune Response." In E. L. Schneider, & J. W. Rowe, (Eds.). Handbook of the Biology of Aging, 4th Edition (pp. 355-392). (New York: Academic Press).

MULTIPLE CHOICE QUESTIONS

1. Cross-sectional research studies conducted prior to 1950 tended to exaggerate the negative physiological effects of aging. One reason for this exaggeration was that

*   a.   these studies failed to control for health factors.
      b.   cross-cultural comparisons were not conducted.
      c.   the instruments used to measure bodily processes were unreliable at that time.
      d.   the studies failed to consider the effects of accidents.

2. One cause of facial wrinkling that tends to occur after age 50 is

    a.   the decreased rate of metabolism in the elderly.
    b.   the poor nutritional habits of many elderly persons.
*   c.   the significant decrease in the fiber collagen on the inside of the skin.
    d.   the significant increase in the blood cholesterol levels of elderly persons.

3. Which of the following is NOT a significant factor in the aging of the skin?

    a.   Heredity.
    b.   Exposure to sunlight.
    c.   Gender.
*   d.   Height and weight.

4. The loss of hair that begins at the temples and gradually spreads to include the entire top of the head is known as

*   a.   male pattern baldness.
    b.   thyroid-related baldness.
    c.   atypical baldness.
    d.   collagen-reduced baldness.

5. One cause of the gradual loss of height among women is

    a.   the delayed effects of childbearing.
*   b.   the loss of bone calcium among women.
    c.   the higher influence of arthritis among elderly women.
    d.   the decrease in muscle strength with age.

6. One reason that the aging process of the skin is more noticeable in women than in men is that

    a.   elderly women have been found to spend more time in the sun than elderly men.
*   b.   women produce less skin oil in old age than men.
    c.   women's cosmetics have been found to exacerbate the aging of the skin,
    d.   none of the above are true.

7. The graying of scalp hair is influenced by

    a.   overall physical health.
    b.   nutritional factors.
    c.   hereditary factors.
    d.   none of the above.

8. One of the effects of metabolic bone disease among women is

    a.   premature menopause.
    b.   loss of height.
    c.   eventual paralysis.
    d.   increased cancer risk.

9. The rate at which the resting body converts food into energy is called

    a.   resting potential.
    b.   basal metabolism.
    c.   resting peristalsis.
    d.   none of the above.

10. The "middle-age spread" which is a ten to fifteen percent weight gain between the ages of 20 and 50, is thought to be caused by the

    a.   increased incidence of diabetes during this age period.
    b.   increased susceptibility to depression during this age period.
    c.   decrease in the basal metabolism rate during these years.
    d.   hormonal changes which occur during this time.

11. One reason that muscles tend to stiffen and heal more slowly with age is that

    a.   the body suffers from an increasing deficiency of iron.
    b.   many elderly people abuse muscle relaxing drugs.
    c.   muscle fiber is gradually replaced with connective tissue.
    d.   none of the above.

12. In general, the resting heart rate tends to

    a.   undergo significant fluctuation throughout adulthood.
    b.   remain about the same throughout adulthood.
    c.   gradually increase with age.
    d.   gradually decrease with age.

13. The brain loses approximately what percent of its weight over the lifespan of an individual?

    a.   1 to 2 percent
*   b.   5 to 10 percent
    c.   15 to 20 percent
    d.   25 percent

14. All of the following are a characteristic of an aging brain except?

*   a.   increased levels of dopamine.
    b.   neuritic plaques.
    c.   lipofuscin.
    d.   neurofibrillary tangles.

15. Which of the following is NOT a benefit of exercise during adulthood?

    a.   muscle deterioration can be slowed.
    b.   the heart and blood vessels increase in efficiency.
    c.   the amount of cholesterol in the blood is reduced.
*   d.   all of the above.

16. The age of peak performance for athletic events varies as a function of

    a.   gender.
    b.   type of event.
    c.   historical time.
*   d.   a plus b.
    e.   all of the above.

17. All of the following are associated with menopause except

    a.   hot flashes.
    b.   increased risk of urinary tract infection.
*   c.   loss of appetite.
    d.   bone loss.

18. The major cause of limited physical activity among the elderly is

*   a.   arthritis.
    b.   gout.
    c.   degenerative muscle functioning.
    d.   Alzheimer's Disease.

19. All of the following are characteristics of the aging brain except

    a.   increased number of neuritic plaques.
    b.   increased number of neurofibrillary tangles.
    c.   decreased amounts of lipofuscin.
    d.   declining amounts of neurotransmitters.

20. Which of the following has <u>NOT</u> been found to be effective in the treatment of arthritis?

    a.   aspirin.
    b.   heat.
    c.   cold.
    d.   valium.

21. Osteoporosis is a common condition among older women. Current findings suggest that the best treatment for this condition is

    a.   diet.
    b.   hormone supplements such as estrogen.
    c.   exercise.
    d.   painkillers such as aspirin.

22. In the past two decades deaths due to which of the following conditions have decreased dramatically?

    a.   heart disease and stroke.
    b.   cancer and heart disease.
    c.   stroke and cancer.
    d.   accidents and cancer.

23. Which of the following describes the accident rate for adults over the age of 65?

    a.   the accident rate increases with age.
    b.   the accident rate decreases with age.
    c.   the accident rate remains the same throughout the lifespan.
    d.   no comprehensive statistics have been kept on accident rates with the elderly.

24. The leading cause of death for individuals 65 years of age and older is

    a.   cancer.
    b.   strokes.
    c.   accidents.
*   d.   heart disease.

25. A group of substances that have been claimed to extend human life by blocking damage to bodily proteins are

*   a.   antioxidants.
    b.   antihypertensives.
    c.   anticoagulants.
    d.   antidementias.

26. When asked to assess their health, approximately what percent of older adults rate their health as good, very good, or excellent?

    a.   9%
    b.   56%
    c.   72%
    d.   92%

27. The genetic cellular theory of aging which posits that aging results from faulty transmission of genetic information within the cell is called

    a.   DNA damage theory.
*   b.   error theory.
    c.   accumulation theory.
    d.   cross-linkage theory.

28. Which group of theories assumes that aging is caused by progressive damage to the organism from its internal and external environment?

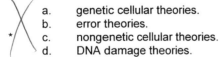

    a.   genetic cellular theories.
    b.   error theories.
*   c.   nongenetic cellular theories.
    d.   DNA damage theories.

29. The theory which assumes aging to be caused by increasing amounts of the insoluble substance lipofuscin is

*   a.   accumulation theory.
      b.   DNA damage theory.
      c.   free radical theory.
      d.   none of the above.

30. The nongenetic cellular theory which attributes aging to the reactions of unstable chemical compounds with surrounding molecules is the

      a.   cross-linkage theory.
      b.   accumulation theory.
      c.   error theory.
*   d.   free radical theory.

31. The group of theories which attributes aging to the wearing out of certain "hot spot" organs is called

      a.   genetic cellular theories.
      b.   nongenetic cellular theories.
*   c.   physiological theories.
      d.   DNA damage theories.

32. The theories that attribute aging to the decrease in the effectiveness of the antibodies are

*   a.   immunological theories.
      b.   accumulation theories.
      c.   cross-linkage theories.
      d.   error theories.

33. All of the following have been shown to be effective anti-aging supplements except

      a.   Ginseng.
      b.   Growth hormone.
      c.   Selenium.
*   d.   None of the above.

34. There is evidence to support the claim that large quantities of which of these dietary supplements is an effective antiaging treatment?

    a.   Vitamin C.
    b.   Selenium.
    c.   Panthothenic acid.
*   d.   none of the above.

35. Which of the following factors has NOT been recognized as an independent factor related to longevity?

    a.   stress.
    b.   marital status.
*   c.   intelligence quotient.
    d.   social relationships.

36. Which of the following behaviors have been recommended as conducive to longer life?

    a.   avoiding long exposure to the sun.
    b.   practicing safe sex.
    c.   maintaining a network of family and friends.
    d.   having a positive attitude.
*   e.   all of the above.

37. Which of the following behaviors has NOT been recommended as conducive to longer life?

    a.   regular health checkups.
    b.   use of seat belts in automobiles.
    c.   moderate use of alcoholic beverages.
*   d.   early retirement.

CHAPTER 4--SENSATION AND PERCEPTION

CHAPTER OBJECTIVES

The purpose of this chapter is to enable students to:

Identify and describe key concepts related to each of the human senses.

Identify key changes in sensory abilities as individuals develop from early adulthood to old age.

Identify factors that may contribute to accelerated sensory decline as individuals age.

Identify ways in which human beings have learned to compensate for age-related sensory declines.

DISCUSSION QUESTIONS

When you observe an old person driving below the speed limit on a road or highway, what attributions do you make regarding their sensory and cognitive abilities? Would you reach the same conclusions about a young person driving below the speed limit?

Can an individual lose their driver's license because of sensory or cognitive declines? What is the procedure in your state for losing one's license? Should driving tests become more stringent in late life?

Given the type of life experience you have had, which of your sensory systems is likely to deteriorate more rapidly than the norm? Why?

How do individuals you know become aware of sensory declines and how do they cope with them?

LEARNING ACTIVITIES

Talk to several adults of different ages and ask them to reflect on sensory changes they have experienced as they grew older and how they dealt with them.

Organize a sensory evaluation experience (e.g. a wine tasting) and invite participants of different ages. Ask each individual to discuss the object being evaluated from a visual, sensory, olfactory, and gustatory perspective. What similarities and differences do you observe among the various age groups?

Invite to class someone with a background in audiology and have them bring an audiometer. Test the hearing of several individuals in class (students and teacher) to demonstrate the wide variability in people's ability to hear.

ADDITIONAL READINGS

Introductory

Kline, D. W., & Scialfa, C. T. 1996. "Visual and Auditory Aging." In J. E. Birren & K. W. Schaie (Eds.), Handbook of the Psychology of Aging, 4th Edition (pp. 181-203) (New York: Academic Press).

Intermediate

Spirduso, W. W. 1995. Physical Dimensions of Aging. (Champaign, IL: Human Kinetics).

Advanced

Schiffman, S. 1996. "Smell and Taste." In J. E. Birren (Ed.). Encyclopedia of Gerontology, Vol. II (pp. 497-504). (New York: Academic Press).

Weisenberger, J. M. 1996. "Touch and Proprioception." In J. E. Birren (Ed.). Enyclopedia of Gerontology, Vol. II: (pp. 591-603). (New York: Academic Press).

MULTIPLE CHOICE QUESTIONS

1. Most visual sensations originate in

*   a.   some external object.
      b.   the lens.
      c.   the iris.
      d.   the photoreceptor cells.

2. The changes in the shape of the lens that enable vision to be focused on both near and distant objects is called

    a.   illumination.
    b.   assimilation.
  *   c.   accommodation.
    d.   incandescence.

3. The change in the iris that is responsible for the amount of light entering the eye is called

    a.   the retinal closure reflex.
    b.   the accommodation principle.
    c.   dark adaptation.
  *   d.   the pupillary reflex.

4. The part of the eye that transforms light energy into nerve impulses is called the

    a.   fovea.
  *   b.   retina.
    c.   sclera.
    d.   optic nerve.

5. The photoreceptors which make color vision possible are called the

  *   a.   cones.
    b.   rods.
    c.   spectral photoreceptors.
    d.   bipolar cells.

6. The process that allows us to shift from daytime to nighttime vision is called

    a.   light adaptation.
  *   b.   dark adaptation.
    c.   stimulus dimming.
    d.   night illumination.

7. The point of intersection between the retina and the optic nerve is called the

    a.   fovea.
    b.   ganglion cell.
  *   c.   blind spot.
    d.   optic pathway.

8. The area of the retina that contains the highest concentration of cones is called the

*   a.   fovea.
     b.   blind spot.
     c.   ciliary muscle.
     d.   bipolar cell.

9. The ability to distinguish one object from another by sight is called

     a.   dark adaptation.
     b.   visual adjustment.
     c.   visual accommodation.
*   d.   visual acuity.

10. Which of the following is NOT an age-related physical change in the eye?

     a.   The pupils dilate less completely.
*   b.   The number of photoreceptors decreases.
     c.   The cornea increases in curvature.
     d.   The lens becomes larger.

11. Which of the following describes the age-related change in dark adaptation?

     a.   We adapt to the dark at a faster rate as we age.
     b.   We completely lose our ability to adapt to dark in old age.
*   c.   We adapt to the dark at a slower rate as we age.
     d.   Our ability to adapt to the dark is unaffected by aging.

12.   The reduced ability to focus on nearby objects is called

     a.   myopia.
     b.   proximal blindness.
     c.   glaucoma.
*   d.   presbyopia.

13. The inability to correctly identify a road sign from a moving automobile would suggest a decline in

*   a.   dynamic visual acuity.
     b.   static visual acuity.
     c.   iconic memory processing.
     d.   none of the above.

14. The percent of elderly persons reporting visual impairments is

    a.   small, less than 3% for those over the age of 65.
    b.   large, more than 30% for those over the age of 65.
*   c.   somewhat higher for men than women.
    d.   about the same for men and women.

15. The change in the ability to see the colors blue, green, and violet after age forty is most likely caused by

    a.   the decrease in the number of cones.
    b.   the decrease in the number of rods.
*   c.   the yellowing of the lens.
    d.   the expansion of the blind spot.

16. The eye disorder that negatively affects vision by inhibiting the passage of light into the eye is called

    a.   glaucoma.
*   b.   cataracts.
    c.   macular degeneration.
    d.   retinal detachment.

17. The eye disorder caused by excessive fluid pressure is called

    a.   cataracts.
    b.   retinal detachment.
*   c.   glaucoma.
    d.   macular degeneration.

18. The leading cause of blindness in the United States is

    a.   congenital blindness.
    b.   glaucoma.
    c.   cataracts.
*   d.   retinal disorders.

19. Which of the following is NOT a disorder of the retina?

    a.   Senile macular degeneration.
*   b.   Cataracts.
    c.   Diabetic retinopathy.
    d.   Retinal detachment.

20. The membrane which separates the middle ear from the inner ear is called the

    a.   eardrum.
    b.   cochlea.
*   c.   oval window.
    d.   basilar membrane.

21. The fluid-filled coiled tube in the inner ear is called the

*   a.   cochlea.
    b.   eardrum.
    c.   auditory nerve.
    d.   oval window.

22. The true auditory receptors, which are located near the basilar membrane, are called

    a.   ossicles.
    b.   semicircular canals.
*   c.   hair cells.
    d.   nerve fibers.

23. The height, or amplitude, of sound waves determines

    a.   pitch.
    b.   resonance.
    c.   harmony.
*   d.   loudness.

24. The frequency of sound waves determines

    a.   loudness.
    b.   resonance.
*   c.   pitch.
    d.   none of the above.

25. The intensity, or loudness, of a sound is measured in

*   a.   decibels.
    b.   hertz.
    c.   B.T.U.'s.
    d.   watts.

26. The percent of persons reporting hearing impairments is

      a.   much higher for males than females.
      b.   much higher than the percent reporting vision impairments.
      c.   highest for the 85 and older group.
*   d.   all of the above are true.

27. The age-related decline in the ability to detect higher-pitched sounds is mainly caused by atrophy of the

      a.   auditory nerve.
*   b.   hair cells.
      c.   eardrum.
      d.   oval window.

28. From 1940 to 1980 the incidence rate of deafness in the population has

      a.   decreased
*   b.   increased
      c.   stayed about the same
      d.   increased only among younger persons

29. The progressive loss of hearing in both ears for high frequency tones is called

*   a.   presbycusis.
      b.   presbyopia.
      c.   conductive hearing loss.
      d.   central auditory impairment.

30. Which of the following has <u>NOT</u> been suggested as a possible cause of presbycusis?

      a.   Long-term exposure to loud noises.
      b.   Improper diet.
*   c.   Trauma to the eardrum.
      d.   Genetic factors.

31. The impairment resulting from the inability of sound waves to travel through the outer and middle ear is called

    a.   presbycusis.
    b.   central auditory impairment.
*   c.   conductive hearing loss.
    d.   none of the above.

32. The inability to understand language despite an intact ability to detect external sound is called

*   a.   central auditory impairment.
    b.   conductive hearing loss.
    c.   presbycusis.
    d.   auditory dementia.

33. The sense of taste is also called

    a.   olfactory discrimination.
    b.   somesthesis.
*   c.   gustation.
    d.   none of the above.

34. One reason for the difficulty in drawing conclusions about age-related changes in taste sensitivity is that

*   a.   the studies involved have not sufficiently controlled
           for health factors.
    b.   the elderly have poor nutritional habits.
    c.   no reliable instruments have been developed to measure taste
           sensitivity.
    d.   the elderly are difficult to recruit for participation in such research.

35. One of the important implications of the National Geographic Scratch and Sniff study is that

*   a.   the odorant added to natural gas should be changed for older persons.
    b.   olfactory sensitivity doesn't show declines until after the age of 70.
    c.   Alzheimer's disease can cause permanent loss of olfactory sensitivity.
    d.   sensitivity to all odors declines at the same rate.

36. Results of research concerning taste preferences and aging have suggested that

    a.   older adults prefer heavily seasoned foods more than younger subjects.
    b.   younger subjects prefer sweeter stimuli more than elderly subjects.
    c.   the taste preferences of older adults did not significantly differ from those of younger subjects.
*   d.   older adults dislike bitter stimuli more than younger subjects.

37. Rather than aging per se, much of the decline in somesthetic sensitivity is thought to be caused by

    a.   poor nutrition.
*   b.   disease and injury.
    c.   decreased activity rate.
    d.   hereditary factors.

38. Research on temperature and aging has indicated significant differences between older adults and younger subjects in which of the following areas?

    a.   Temperature sensitivity.
    b.   Temperature preferences.
*   c.   Ability to cope with extreme temperatures.
    d.   No differences were found in any area of temperature research.

39. Although the available data on changes with age in pain sensitivity are equivocal, we do know that

*   a.   the frequency and intensity of chronic pain increases in late life.
    b.   older persons report less pain than younger persons.
    c.   older and younger persons report equal levels of pain.
    d.   older adults have been taught not to acknowledge feel of pain.

40. The sensation generated by the body that lets you know the location of your limbs in space is called

    a.   gustation.
    b.   infallibility.
    c.   signal detection.
*   d.   proproception

41. Declines in proprioception and kinesthetic function in the elderly may contribute to

   a. cognitive declines in late life
   b. increases in auto accidents in late life
 * c. falls in the elderly
   d. all of the above.

CHAPTER 5-- MEMORY

CHAPTER OBJECTIVES

The purpose of this chapter is to enable students to:

Identify and define key concepts related to memory.

Identify and describe methodological difficulties in studying the relationship between aging and memory.

Identify important conceptualizations of memory and how they have been used to guide the investigation of age-related differences in memory.

Understand the functional consequences of age-related declines in memory.

DISCUSSION QUESTIONS

Compare and contrast at least two different ways in which memory has been proposed to operate, and explain how these frameworks have helped in the understanding of age differences in memory.

List all reasons why an older adult might perform more poorly than a younger adult in a memory experiment.

To what extent do people believe that their memory declines with age? Is this related to actual memory performance?

Discuss the possibility that we have a permanent record of everything that ever happens to us, and that the limits in memory are associated with accessing that information and not with its storage.

LEARNING ACTIVITIES

Meet with educators in an over 60s program. Find out what subjects or topics are of most interest to those enrolled in the program. What teaching techniques have they found to be most useful or appropriate for the over 60 learner? What characteristics do they use to describe the over 60 learner? Based on the information you gather from these educators, how would you describe the similarities and differences between the over 60 learner and students in your class?

Visit an intergenerational program, and ask the staff what they see as similarities and differences in learning between older and younger participants. Does the staff find it necessary to make special arrangements for either group in order to help participants feel more comfortable and involved? If possible, spend some time observing interactions between older and younger participants. Do your observations agree or disagree with the information provided by the staff? Based on the information gathered during your visit, how would you describe the learning of older and younger participants?

Ask older relatives about any reported difficulties with memory, ranging from problems with locating familiar objects (e.g. keys, glasses), remembering where one parked one's car, remembering the details of a book or movie, to remembering early events in one's life. Is there a pattern in which some types of memory seem to be preserved better than others?

Interview people of different ages and ask about their learning interests at different stages in their lives. Also ask how their capacity to learn has changed over time; for example, has learning become easier or more difficult? Based on the information you gather, what conclusions would you draw about the nature of learning throughout the adult life span?

ADDITIONAL READINGS

Introductory

Skinner, B. F. 1983. "Intellectual Self-Management in Old Age." American Psychologist: 38, 239-244.

Intermediate

Schacter, D.L. 1986. Searching for Memory: The Brain, the Mind, and the Past. (New York: Basic Books).

Salthouse, T.A. 1991. Theorietical Perspectives in Cognitive Aging. (Mahwah, N.J.: Lawrence Erlbaum Associates).

Advanced

Kausler, D.H., 1994. Learning and Memory in Normal Aging. (San Diego: Academic Press).

Craik, F.I.M. & Salthouse, T.A. (Eds.) In press. Handbook of Aging and Cognition (2nd Ed.), (Mahwah, N.J.: Lawrence Erlbaum Associates).

MULTIPLE CHOICE QUESTIONS

1. The process-oriented approach to research on age differences in memory is considered analogous to

    a.   a doctor conducting exploratory surgery.
    b.   a stock market analyst trying to identify a systematic pattern. underlying changes in stock prices.
*   c.   an automobile mechanic attempting to determine which part is defective.
    d.   a pilot relying on pre-specified procedures when flying an airplane.

2. Research results from the Wechsler Memory Scale suggest that age differences are

    a.   greater for meaningful paragraphs than for unrelated words.
    b.   greater for unrelated words than for meaningful paragraphs.
    c.   greater for face recognition than for logical memory.
*   d.   about the same for meaningful paragraphs and for unrelated words.

3. Results from several different studies suggest that age differences are

*   a.   about the same for verbal and spatial material.
    b.   greater for verbal material than for spatial material.
    c.   greater for spatial material than for verbal material.
    d.   greater for verbal material except when the spatial material involves meaningful pictures.

4. Prospective memory refers to

    a.   memory for incidental but potentially relevant information.
*   b.   remembering to do something in the future.
    c.   anticipating what might need to be remembered later.
    d.   memory as used in other cognitive activities.

5. Reality monitoring is related to

    a.   metamemory because the individual fails to become aware of his/her memory.
*   b.   source memory because the individual fails to recognize the source of his/her memory.
    c.   psychopathology because the individual is incapable of recognizing reality.
    d.   procedural memory because the individual lacks procedures for successfully.
        monitoring reality.

6. Proactive and retroactive interference refer, respectively, to interference attributable to

    a.   material presented after and before the to-be-remembered material
*   b.   material presented before and after the to-be-remembered material
    c.   material that facilitates or impairs retention of the to-be-remembered material
    d.   active versus inactive processes during remembering

7. A research procedure used to investigate the interference interpretation of age differences in memory involves

*   a.   comparing memory for items after being exposed to a different set of items.
    b.   comparing memory tested by recognition procedures with that tested by recall procedures.
    c.   comparing memory for material learned with and without interfering mediators.
    d.   comparing memory for material presented directly versus indirectly.

8. The information about the plot of your favorite movie is most likely to be stored in your

    a.   sensory memory.
*   b.   secondary memory.
    c.   primary memory.
    d.   core memory.

9. Two characteristics that can be used to distinguish sensory and primary memory are

   a.   the modality of the information and how information is maintained.
   b.   the modality of the information and the quality of the representation.
   c.   the duration of the information and the modality of the information.
   d.   the capacity of the storage and the duration of the information.

10. The ability to recall items from the beginning of a list most easily is a phenomenon known as the

   a.   recency effect.
   b.   serial effect.
   c.   paired associate effect.
   d.   primacy effect.

11. Subjects given a list of items to learn tend to have the MOST difficulty recalling

   a.   items at the beginning of the list.
   b.   items in the middle of the list.
   c.   items at the end of the list.
   d.   all items with equal frequency.

12. One of the problems with investigating relations between age and tertiary memory is

   a.   the information may have been forgotten.
   b.   it is difficult to be certain that the information has not been rehearsed during the interval.
   c.   changes may have occurred in the external environment.
   d.   memories might change qualitatively as well as quantitatively.

13. Research by the psychologist Harry Bahrick has been important for

   a.   establishing that people remember faces better than names.
   b.   establishing that some information can be retained at relatively high levels for decades.
   c.   establishing that people forget information more rapidly when distracted shortly.
        after presentation of the information.
   d.   establishing that material is better remembered when it is presented in two modalities than in one.

14. Which of the following statements is most true?

      a.   age decrements do not occur for retrieval.
*   b.   age decrements are greater for retrieval than for storage.
      c.   age decrements are greater for storage than for retrieval.
      d.   age decrements do not occur in encoding.

15. The stages and stores least affected by increased age are

      a.   encoding; secondary memory.
      b.   retrieval; primary memory.
*   c.   storage; remote (tertiary) memory.
      d.   encoding; working memory.

16. The levels of processing model is most useful in focusing on _____ changes with aging.

      a.   quantitative.
*   b.   qualitative.
      c.   semantic memory.
      d.   working memory.

17. Names and definitions of words are part of _____ memory, whereas skills and habits are part of _____ memory.

      a.   episodic; semantic
      b.   explicit; implicit
      c.   mnemonic; heuristic
*   d.   declarative; procedural

18. Playing a piano piece from memory retrieves a(n)

*   a.   procedural memory.
      b.   episodic memory.
      c.   semantic memory.
      d.   metamemory.

19. General knowledge is considered to be part of

*   a.   semantic memory.
      b.   verbal memory.
      c.   episodic memory.
      d.   implicit memory.

20. The type of memory proposed by Tulving, which is a record of experiences in terms of time and place is called

    a.   semantic memory.
    b.   procedural memory.
    c.   sensory memory.
*   d.   episodic memory.

21. The type of memory proposed by Tulving, which retains our general knowledge about words, numbers, and symbols is called

*   a.   semantic memory.
    b.   procedural memory.
    c.   episodic memory.
    d.   eidetic memory.

22. The recollection of your high school graduation would involve the use of

    a.   semantic memory.
    b.   procedural memory.
*   c.   episodic memory.
    d.   serial memory.

23. The recollection that paper is made from wood would involve tapping the contents of

    a.   procedural memory.
    b.   flashbulb memory.
*   c.   semantic memory.
    d.   episodic memory.

24. A possible implication of research on age differences in implicit or indirect memory is

    a.   with increased age the amount of explicit knowledge increases but implicit knowledge decreases.
    b.   with increased age the amount of explicit knowledge decreases but implicit knowledge increases.
*   c.   people retain much more information than they are consciously aware.
    d.   people remember more information when it is learned implicitly than when it is learned explicitly.

25. One possible definition of implicit memory is that it refers to

    *   a.   effects of past experience evident without any conscious attempt at recollection.
        b.   memory that people have implicitly, but that is not always obvious.
        c.   memory that is revealed by conscious attempts at remembering.
        d.   memory that is revealed while the individual is unconscious.

26. Working memory is closely related to

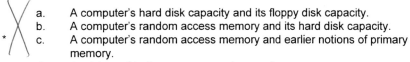

        a.   A computer's hard disk capacity and its floppy disk capacity.
        b.   A computer's random access memory and its hard disk capacity.
    *   c.   A computer's random access memory and earlier notions of primary memory.
        d.   A mixture of tertiary memory and secondary memory.

27. The three criteria often used to determine whether a memory problem is serious are

        a.   If the individual loses his/her keys more than twice in one week, forgets to eat more than one meal in a given day, and is concerned about his/her memory.
    *   b.   If the individual scores at or below the 5th percentile for his/her age, is impaired in everyday functioning, and the level of performance has deteriorated from an earlier period.
        c.   If the individual performs at or below the 5th percentile level for his/her age on a test of memory for unrelated words, on a test of memory for faces, and on a test of memory for meaningful paragraphs.
        e.   If the individual reports losing objects more than twice in one month, has difficulty recalling the names of friends and relatives, and frequently forgets the topic of a conversation immediately after finishing it.

28. The two major goals of most memory intervention research are

        a.   to improve memory for faces and names of friends and relatives.
    *   b.   to increase the memory functioning of older adults or to reduce the magnitude of age differences in memory.
        b.   to reduce the frequency of forgetting where objects were placed, and improve memory for names.
        c.   to increase confidence in one's memory, and improve accuracy of memory.

CHAPTER 6--INTELLIGENCE AND COGNITION

CHAPTER OBJECTIVES

The purpose of this chapter is to enable students to:

Identify and define key concepts related to intelligence and cognition.

Identify and explain major difficulties encountered in measuring intelligence, cognition, and wisdom.

Describe the pattern of age-related differences in intellectual and cognitive performance.

Describe how various interpretations of age-related differences in cognition have been investigated.

Describe how different researchers have come to define and study wisdom.

DISCUSSION QUESTIONS

Explain the limitations of using a psychometric approach to measuring adult intelligence and why, given such limitations, this approach is still used as a basis for studying the effects of aging on intelligence.

Identify a dimension of intelligence and discuss methods by which it is measured, and how it is affected by aging.

Explain how the age relations in cognition might differ when assessed by cross-sectional versus longitudinal methods.

Explain the difference between convergent and divergent thinking; give an example of each.

How are age and creative productivity related?

What makes a person wise? To what extent is wisdom a characteristic of older persons?

LEARNING ACTIVITIES

Ask people of different ages to define intelligence and wisdom. Compare and contrast the various definitions. Indicate whether you agree or disagree with the definitions and why.

To what extent do you think cognitive abilities are important in everyday life? Try to identify situations that place great importance on fluid abilities and on crystallized abilities.

Is there a paradox that the research evidence suggests that some types of cognitive abilities, including aspects of decision making, tend to decline with increased age and yet most of the important decision-makers in society tend to be older adults? Try to think of explanations of this apparent inconsistency.

Investigate the life course of a well-known, well-recognized creative person. What was this person doing at different stages in his/her life? What does this person's life seem to indicate about the relationship between creativity and aging?

Investigate the ways in which "ordinary" people channel or express their creativity at different stages in their life.

Ask young and old persons to identify individuals whom they consider wise. Explain why specific persons were selected to be on this list.

ADDITIONAL READINGS

Intermediate

Baltes, P.B., & Staudinger, U.M. 1993. "The Search for a Psychology of Wisdom." Current Directions in Psychological Science: 2, 75-80.

Schaie, K.W. 1993. "The Seattle Longitudinal Studies of Adult Intelligence." Current Directions in Psychological Science: 2, 171-175.

Simonton, D.K. 1990. "Creativity and Wisdom in Aging." In J.E. Birren & K.W. Schaie   (Eds.), Handbook of the Psychology of Aging, 3rd Edition (pp. 320-329). (San Diego: Academic Press).

Advanced

Horn, J.L., Hofer, S.M. 1992. "Major Abilities and Development in the Adult Period." In R. Sternberg & C.A. Berg (Eds.), Intellectual Development (pp. 44-99). (New York: Cambridge University Press).

Salthouse, T. A. 1991. Theoretical Perspectives in Cognitive Aging. (Hillsdale, N.J: Lawrence Erlbaum Associates).

MULTIPLE CHOICE QUESTIONS

1. Reliance on objective and standardized procedures to assess level of intelligence is a primary characteristic of what approach?

    a. functional assessment.
    * b. psychometric.
    c. differential.
    d. information processing.

2. An important disadvantage of the psychometric approach to intelligence is

    a. the tests tend to have low levels of reliability.
    b. relatively little data are available from large samples.
    * c. there is still little consensus on what intelligence means.
    d. the tests have little or no validity.

3. One of the major findings from the analyses of the WWI Army Alpha data was

    a. the age-related increases were more pronounced for people with more education.
    b. the age-related increases were more pronounced for officers than for enlisted men.
    * c. average scores decreased before age 50.
    d. average scores decreased only after age 50.

4. The section of the Wechsler Adult Intelligence Scale which focuses on the store of general knowledge is called the

    * a. Verbal Scale.
    b. Performance Scale.
    c. Digit Symbol Subtest.
    d. General Recall Subtest.

47

5. IQ scores derived from the Wechsler scales

    a. reflect equal amounts of genetic and environmental influences.
*   b. have the same average at each age range.
    c. are based on weighting knowledge twice as much as creativity.
    d. largely represent acquired abilities.

6. Which intelligence tests were the earliest, the most popular, and the one used in the Seattle Longitudinal Study?

    a. Wechsler, Army Alpha, Primary Mental Abilities.
    b. Wechsler, Primary Mental Abilities, Army Alpha.
*   c. Army Alpha, Wechsler, Primary Mental Abilities.
    d. Army Alpha, Primary Mental Abilities, Wechsler.

7. One ability showing stability or increment in old age is

    a. general intelligence.
    b. spatial reasoning.
*   c. vocabulary.
    d. fluid ability.

8. Fluid intelligence refers to

    a. ability to apply learned experience and knowledge.
    b. intelligence that is not fixed or static.
    c. intelligence that is affected by cultural biases.
*   d. the capacity to process novel information.

9. The capacity to use unique kinds of thinking in the solving of unfamiliar problems is known as

    a. crystallized intelligence.
*   b. fluid intelligence.
    c. plastic intelligence.
    d. native intelligence.

10. The knowledge that has been acquired through education and acculturation is called

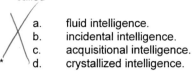

- a. fluid intelligence.
- b. incidental intelligence.
- c. acquisitional intelligence.
- * d. crystallized intelligence.

11. According to the text, estimates of age differences in cognitive functioning are

- * a. probably similar in cross-sectional and longitudinal comparisons.
- c. larger in cross-sectional comparisons than in longitudinal comparisons.
- d. larger in longitudinal comparisons than in cross-sectional comparisons.
- e. greater in time-lag comparisons than in longitudinal comparisons.

12. A syllogism is an example of

- a. spatial integration ability.
- b. perceptual closure ability.
- * c. deductive reasoning ability.
- d. inductive reasoning ability.

13. The 20 Questions Game and the Raven's Progressive Matrices are examples of

- a. decision making and spatial integration abilities.
- * b. decision making and inductive reasoning abilities.
- c. creativity and decision making abilities.
- d. concept formation and deductive reasoning abilities.

14. One way that creativity has been measured is with

- a. implicit thinking tests.
- b. convergent thinking tests.
- * c. divergent thinking tests.
- d. integrative thinking tests.

49

15. A solution to a significant problem of society that is original, unusual, ingenious, and relevant mainly involves the use of

    a.   convergent thinking.
    b.   plasticity.
*   c.   creativity.
    d.   crystallized intelligence.

16. Solving a problem by narrowing down many possibilities and arriving at one correct answer involves the use of

    a.   divergent thinking.
*   b.   convergent thinking.
    c.   trial and error.
    d.   crystallized intelligence.

17. One of the reasons why wisdom has been difficult to investigate is

    a.   most wise people have already died.
    b.   very few wise people exist.
*   c.   there is no generally accepted criterion for evaluating wisdom.
    d.   wisdom cannot be distinguished from general intelligence.

18. Although declining health has often been assumed to be a cause of age-related declines in cognitive functioning, this interpretation has not been supported because

*   a.   age trends in cognitive functioning have been found to be very similar for people who vary in level of self-reported health.
    b.   people with higher levels of objective health perform better in most cognitive tests than people of lower health levels.
    c.   health status does not really decline until people are over the age of 75.
    d.   health status is unrelated to cognitive functioning.

19. According to the text, level of education does not appear to be a major factor responsible for age differences in cognitive functioning because

    a.   there are currently little or no age differences in average amount of education completed.
    b.   higher amounts of education are often associated with lower levels of cognitive functioning.
    c.   people with greater amounts of education exhibit little or no age-related decline in measures of cognitive functioning
*   d.   the age trends in cognitive functioning are very similar for people with different amounts of education.

20. The discovery that successive generations tend to score higher on many cognitive tests than earlier generations is an example of

    a.   cultural drift.
    b.   the benefits of early childhood television viewing.
*   c.   a time-lag effect.
    d.   a negative environmental bias effect.

21. One important type of evidence that is inconsistent with cultural change or cohort interpretations of age differences in cognition is

*   a.   research with animals.
    b.   research comparing age trends in different cohorts.
    c.   research comparing early and late generations when they were at the same age.
    d.   research with culture-free tests of knowledge and general information.

22. Support for a disuse interpretation of age differences in cognition would be provided by

    a.   a finding that people with more experience in a domain exhibit higher levels of performance than people with less experience.
    b.   a finding that the age-related declines are greater in familiar tasks and activities than in unfamiliar ones.
    c.   a finding that people who have received additional experience with a task tend to perform better than people without that experience.
*   d.   a finding that people who have considerable experience within a domain tend to have smaller age-related declines in relevant tasks within that domain than people with less experience.

CHAPTER 7--PERSONALITY AND AGING

CHAPTER OBJECTIVES

The purpose of this chapter is to enable students to:

Identify and define key concepts related to personality and aging.

Identify methodological issues that make it difficult to study the relationship between personality and aging.

Compare and contrast alternative stage theories of adulthood and personality development.

Identify and describe key personality traits that have been studied in order to explain personality development in adulthood.

Describe the key features of new synthetic theories of life-span development.

Articulate the general principles regulating development across the life course.

Describe the life course theory of control of Schulz and Heckhausen.

DISCUSSION QUESTIONS

What are the advantages and disadvantages of studying personality in the laboratory, clinical setting, and field setting?

Review the seven stages of adult development suggested by Gould. Do the issues he associates with your current age accurately reflect how you feel?

Think about the personalities of various members of your family. What are some of the similarities and differences? What factors do you think contributed to these similarities and differences?

Identify important historical events that have helped to shape your personality. Compare and contrast how these same historical events affected other members of your class.

LEARNING ACTIVITIES

Characterize your parents' personalities now and at different stages in their lives. In what ways have their personalities changed and stayed the same? Talk with other relatives (e.g. grandparents, aunts, uncles) in your family who have known your parents over the years. Get their perspectives on your parents' personalities.

Levinson suggests that men in their early 40s experience a mid-life transition, often referred to as a "mid-life crisis." Talk with several men in their 40s and/or 50s to determine whether they experienced such a transition. If so, find out what issues they were dealing with; how they resolved these issues; how long the transition lasted; what brought the transition to an end. If they did not experience this type of transition, find out if, as Costa and McCrae suggest, these individuals do not tend to experience crises throughout their lives. (Note: Although Levinson's theory is based on his study of men, you might want to talk with women in this age range and compare their responses to those of the men.)

ADDITIONAL READINGS

Introductory

Roberto, K. A., & Stroes, J. 1995. "Grandchildren and Grandparents: Roles, Influences, and Relationships." In J. Hendricks (Ed.), The Ties of Later Life (pp. 141-153). (Amityville, NY: Baywood).

Intermediate

Kivnick, H. Q., & Sinclair, H. M. 1996. "Grandparenthood." In J. E. Birren (Ed.). Encyclopedia of gerontology, Vol. 1 (pp. 611-623). (New York: Academic Press).

Advanced

Ryff, C. D. 1991. "Possible Selves in Adulthood and Old Age: A Tale of Shifting Horizons." Psychology and Aging: 6, 286-295.

Hunter, S., & Sundel, M. (Eds.) 1989. Midlife Myths: Issues, Findings, and Practice Implications. (Newbury Park, CA: Sage Publications).

MULTIPLE CHOICE QUESTIONS

1. A comprehensive definition of personality would argue that it includes all of the following attributes of an individual except

    a. physical.
*   b. intellectual.
    c. social.
    d. mental.

2. Which of the following was <u>NOT</u> listed in the text as a methodological problem in studies of aging and personality?

    a.   Weaknesses of chronological age as a measure of aging.
    b.   Influence of major life experiences on personality.
*   c.   Difficulty in the recruitment of a heterogenous elderly population.
    d.   Mathematical difficulties that hinder measurement of psychological change.

3. One of the criticisms that has been leveled against the laboratory research of personality is that

    a.   it is subjective and uncontrolled.
*   b.   it is artificial and unrealistic.
    c.   psychopathology is difficult to simulate in the laboratory.
    d.   laboratory researchers disregard data that contradict their hypotheses.

4. The organized distinctive pattern of behavior that characterizes a particular individual is a common definition of

    a.   traits.
    b.   stage theory.
    c.   type theory.
*   d.   personality.

5. According to Levinson's stage theory, the transitional period between adolescence and early adulthood is called

*   a.   leaving the family.
    b.   entering the adult world.
    c.   settling down.
    d.   becoming one's own man.

6. According to Levinson's stage theory, the exploration of various occupational and interpersonal roles takes place during which stage?

    a.   leaving the family.
    b.   becoming one's own man.
    c.   settling down.
*   d.   entering the adult world.

7. Gould derived his set of situational stages of adulthood from

    a.   interviews.
*   b.   clinical observation.
    c.   laboratory research.
    d.   anonymous questionnaires.

8. The psychosexual stages of development were first postulated by

    a.   Buhler.
    b.   Jung.
    c.   Erikson.
*   d.   Freud.

9. Which of these theorists would most likely argue that a person's personality is firmly established well before adulthood?

    a.   Erikson.
*   b.   Freud.
    c.   Levinson.
    d.   Gould.

10. The emphasis of Erik Erikson's stage theory could be described as

*   a.   psychosocial.
    b.   psychosexual.
    c.   physiological.
    d.   situational.

11. Loevinger's focus on the ego as the chief organizer of personality is derived from

*   a.   Erikson.
        b.   Levinson.
        c.   Gould.
        d.   Freud.

12. According to Loevinger, each of the following is important in personality development except

        a.   character development.
        b.   interpersonal style.
*   c.   unconscious drives.
        d.   cognitive style.

13. The turning point that occurs in each of the eight stages hypothesized by Erik Erikson is called a

        a.   plateau.
        b.   fixation.
        c.   catastrophe.
*   d.   crisis.

14. The personality theorist who defined adulthood psychologically, rather than chronologically, was

*   a.   Harry Stack Sullivan.
        b.   Henry Murray.
        c.   Daniel Levinson.
        d.   Gordon Allport.

15. A theory of personality that stresses the major biological phases during one's life was proposed by

        a.   Loevenger.
*   b.   Buhler.
        c.   Gould.
        d.   Sheehy.

16. According to the personality theory of Carl Jung, the values of middle-aged people shift in nature to become more

    a.   materialistic.
    b.   egocentric.
    c.   spiritual.
    d.   identity-oriented.

17. Which of the following was <u>NOT</u> mentioned in the text as a criticism of stage theories?

    a.   The existence of a midlife crisis has not been verified empirically.
    b.   The theories tend to be too complex for the general public to understand.
    c.   Research studies have failed to obtain adequate and representative samples.
    d.   Individual differences make widespread generalizability difficult.

18. The specific components that initiate and guide consistent forms of behavior are known as

    a.   moods.
    b.   dispositions.
    c.   motivations.
    d.   traits.

19. Gordon Allport estimated the range of the number of personality traits to be between

    a.   50 and 100.
    b.   350 and 500.
    c.   1000 and 2000.
    d.   4000 and 5000.

20. According to Allport, the general aspects of personality which can be used to compare adults with one another are called

    a.   common traits.
    b.   personal traits.
    c.   universal stages.
    d.   situational stages.

21. The 550-item, true-false questionnaire which is the most commonly used personality test among older adults is the

- a. Thematic Apperception Test.
- b. Rorshach Test.
- c. Bender Gestalt Test.
- * d. Minnesota Multiphasic Personality Inventory.

22. The projective technique in which the subject is asked to make up a story to accompany presented ambiguous pictures is called the

- a. Rorschach Test.
- * b. Thematic Apperception Test.
- c. 16 PF Inventory.
- d. NEO Inventory.

23. The measure of personality developed by McCrae and Costa which is based on a five trait model is called the

- */ a. NEO Inventory.
- b. MMPI.
- c. 16 PF.
- d. TAT Method.

24. All of the following are major traits assessed by the NEO except

- a. Neuroticism.
- b. Extraversion.
- c. Internality.
- d. Openness to Experience.

25. The most serious criticism of trait theories concerns the issue of

- a. reliability.
- b. construct validity.
- c. circularity of definitions.
- d. nonsignificant correlations.

26. One contribution of trait theory that was mentioned in the text is that

   *   a.   it has provided many useful descriptions of human behavior.
         b.   cognitive theories of personality have been disproven.
         c.   traits have been shown to change drastically as a
                 result of aging.
         d.   it has provided in-depth explanations of behavior.

27. Rotter's term for the trait concerning the belief about the source of rewards and punishment was termed

         a.   primary reinforcement.
         b.   extraversion.
   *   c.   locus of control.
         d.   field dependence.

28. Research has demonstrated that individuals oriented toward an internal locus of control tend to have a higher level of psychological adjustment, except possibly

         a.   in elderly populations.
         b.   in cross-sectional studies.
   *   c.   in institutionalized settings.
         d.   in college populations.

29. One possible reason for the conflicting research results concerning locus of control and aging is that

         a.   researchers have had difficulty accurately measuring locus of control.
         b.   the studies involved have not used representative samples.
         c.   longitudinal studies have not been conducted.
   *   d.   locus of control appears to involve a number of different dimensions.

30. Older people are more likely to be more external on which of the following dimensions?

         a.   social relationships.
         b.   work.
   *   c.   intelligence.
         d.   wisdom.

31. Research concerning aging and introversion-extraversion have suggested that

      a.   this trait does not actually exist.
*   b.   no firm conclusion can be drawn based on the existing data.
      c.   adults become more extraverted as they grow older.
      d.   this trait is influenced by cohort factors.

32. Which of the following was <u>NOT</u> mentioned in the text as a factor that might influence activity level in adults?

      a.   educational variables.
      b.   physiological variables.
      c.   cultural variables.
      d.   psychological variables.

33. One of the important recent developments in gerontology are synthetic models of life-span development. They are characterized by

      a.   focusing on development from infancy to old age.
      b.   considering multiple domains such as physical, social, and cognitive functioning.
      c.   emphasizing both individual and societal factors shaping development
*   d.   all of the above.

34. All of the following represent general principles regulating development across the life-span except

      a.   diversity.
*   b.   regulation.
      c.   selectivity.
      d.   compensation.

35. According to the text, one of the important tasks of early development is to

*   a.   selectively invest time and energy resources in order to realize one's developmental potential.
      b.   become proficient and highly skilled in a few areas of functioning as early as possible.
      c.   ignore failures.
      d.   discover the one thing you are best at.

36. An important developmental challenge is overcoming which of the following types of experiences

    a.   normative developmental failures.
    b.   developmental declines in late life.
    c.   random negative events.
*   d.   all of the above.

37. According to the life-span theory of Schulz and Heckhausen, the central construct critical in understanding life-span development is

    a.   habituation.
*   b.   primary control.
    c.   coping.
    d.   adaptation.

38. The major difference between primary and secondary control, according to Schulz and Heckhausen, is that the latter

    a.   is typically a cognitive process as opposed to an action engaging the environment.
    b.   is important but less critical for the development of the organism.
    c.   is particularly important in helping humans cope with failures and declines.
*   d.   all of the above.

CHAPTER 8--RELATIONSHIPS AND INTERPERSONAL BEHAVIOR

CHAPTER OBJECTIVES

The purpose of this chapter is to enable students to:

Identify and define key concepts relevant to relationships and interpersonal behavior and aging.

Differentiate between myths/stereotypes and scientific evidence about aging and interpersonal relationships.

Compare and contrast alternative theories of aging and interpersonal behavior; describe the contributions and limitations of each.

Describe gender-related changes in sexuality that occur with aging.

Differentiate between statistically and temporally normative life events.

Identify factors that contribute to the formation of friendships.

DISCUSSION QUESTIONS

How would you characterize your relationship with your parents over the last 18 - 20 years? Describe how your relationship has changed, and how it has stayed the same.

At each stage in your life, what relationships have been the most significant to you and why? What types of relationships do you think will be most significant in future decades?

To what extent is your behavior motivated by a desire to establish and maintain relationships with others? What does this tell you about the importance of relationships to human beings?

Who are your three best same-sex friends and three best opposite-sex friends? What is the basis of these friendships? What factors contributed to your initial attraction to each person? Have these factors remained important in the relationship or changed over time?

LEARNING ACTIVITIES

Identify major life events that have occurred within your family (e.g., marriages, birth of children, retirement, deaths). Were these events temporally normative and statistically normative? Compare the life events of your family with those of your classmates' families. Overall, would you characterize your class as temporally and statistically normative? Why or why not?

Interview a couple who has been married for 20 years or more. What attracted them in the first place; what has kept them together; how has their relationship changed over time? What factors have contributed to the length of their marriage? What advice would they give to a newly married couple about making a marriage successful? Compare the information you gather through your interview with that gathered by your classmates. Identify similarities and differences among these relationships.

What is the role of grandparents within your family? After writing down your perceptions of your grandparents' role, interview them. How do they perceive their role? In what ways are their perceptions similar to or different from yours? What do they like about their role; what don't they like?

ADDITIONAL READINGS

Introductory

Lauer, R. H., Lauer, J. C., & Kerr, S. T. 1995. "The Long-Term Marriage: Perceptions of Stability and Satisfaction." In J. Hendricks (Ed.), The Ties of Later Life (pp. 35-41). (Amityville, NY: Baywood).

Intermediate

Adams, R. G., & Blieszner, R. 1995. "Aging Well With Friends and Family. Special Issue: Aging Well in Contemporary Society." American Behavioral Scientist: 39, 209-224.

Carstensen, L. L. In press. "A Life Span Approach to Social Motivation. In J. Heckhausen & C. Dweck (Eds.), Motivation and Self-Regulation Across the Life Span. (London: Cambridge University Press).

Advanced

Heckhausen, J., & Schulz, R. 1995. "A Life-Course Theory of Control." Psychological Review: 102, 284-304.

Schulz, R., & Heckhausen, J. 1996. "A Life-Span Model of Successful Aging." American Psychologist: 51, 702-714.

MULTIPLE CHOICE QUESTIONS

1. Graduation from high school at the age of 40 would be considered which type of event?

    a.   temporally normative.
*   b.   temporally non-normative.
    c.   statistically normative.
    d.   statistically non-normative.

2. Being elected president of the United States would be considered which type of an event?

    a.   temporally normative.
    b.   temporally non-normative.
    c.   statistically normative.
*   d.   statistically non-normative.

3. Whether an event is temporally normative or non-normative depends exclusively on

    a.   the frequency with which it occurs.
    b.   validation from society.
    c.   the individual's perception of the event.
*   d.   the age at which it occurs.

4. Which of the following was <u>NOT</u> mentioned in the text as an important factor in the formation of adult friendship?

    a.   Self-disclosure.
    b.   Physical attractiveness.
    c.   Intelligence and competence.
*   d.   Opposite personalities.

5. In order to qualify as a friendship, the relationship between two people must be

     a.   voluntary.
     b.   mutual.
     c.   flexible.
     d.   terminable.
*   e.   all of the above.

6. According to Matthews, all of the following are common friendship styles except the following

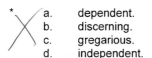

*   a.   dependent.
     b.   discerning.
     c.   gregarious.
     d.   independent.

7. Research on friendship and aging has suggested that the number of close adult friendships

*   a.   remains relatively stable throughout the lifespan.
     b.   increases with age.
     c.   decreases with age.
     d.   undergoes the most fluctuation during old age.

8. Research studies have yielded evidence suggesting that, after age 55, the frequency of contact with close friends

*   a.   is significantly related to overall life satisfaction.
     b.   declines drastically due to poor health.
     c.   increases dramatically due to higher amounts of leisure time.
     d.   is higher for males than for females.

9. The type of love that is highlighted by affection for the people closely involved in our lives is called

     a.   D-love.
     b.   passionate love.
*   c.   companionate love.
     d.   casual love.

10. According to Abraham Maslow, the type of love that is characterized by the selfish need to receive love from others is called

    a.   B-love.
    b.   S-love.
    c.   D-love.
    d.   passionate love.

11. In Maslow's theory, the type of love that is nonpossessive, giving, and honest is called

    a.   D-love.
*   b.   B-love.
    c.   companionate love.
    d.   passionate love.

12. According to Erich Fromm, unhealthy experiences in later life can cause humans to revert to the infant state of

*   a.   narcissism.
    b.   depression.
    c.   helplessness.
    d.   masochism.

13. In Rubin's psychometric study of love, which was explained in the text, one difference that was found between men and women was that

    a.   men liked their love partners more than women did.
*   b.   women liked their love partners more than men did.
    c.   men loved their same-sex friends more than women did.
    d.   women had more negative feelings about their dating partners than men did.

14. In the Lauer et al. studies of enduring marriages, which was discussed in the text, both men and women <u>most often</u> cited which of the following statements as a reason for their enduring love relationships?

    a.   We agree on a philosophy of life.
    b.   My spouse is my best friend.
    c.   We laugh together.
    d.   Marriage is important to social stability.

15. The time that a married couple spends together after the last child leaves home, up until the death of a spouse is called

    a.   the golden years.
    b.   the empty nest.
    c.   the pre-retirement years.
    d.   middle age.

16. The amount of time that married couples spend in the empty nest phase has

    a.   increased in the last few decades.
    b.   decreased in the last few decades.
    c.   stayed about the same.

17. All of the following factors have contributed to the lengthening of the empty nest phase except

    a.   smaller families.
    b.   closer spacing of children.
    c.   longer life span.
    d.   increased divorce rate.

18. When an older person becomes seriously ill or disabled, care is most often provided by

    a.   hospitals.
    b.   nursing homes.
    c.   family members.
    d.   home care professionals.

19. Both men and women report that the major reasons marriages end are

     a.   communication problems and basic unhappiness.
     b.   emotional abuse and financial problems.
     c.   sexual problems.
*   d.   all of the above.

20. Remarriage rates are lowest for

     a.   older men.
*   b.   older women.
     c.   younger men.
     d.   younger women.

21. Persons who remarry late as opposed to early in life tend to have

*   a.   better marriages.
     b.   worse marriages.
     c.   higher divorce rates.
     d.   less stable marriages.

22. The factor which seems to most influence the division of household respon-
sibilities between the husband and wife is

     a.   religious affiliation.
     b.   educational level.
*   c.   the presence of children.
     d.   cultural background.

23. Few age-related conclusions have been drawn about marriage and divorce
because

*   a.   it is difficult to separate aging effects from personality, motivation, and
           other cohort effects.
     b.   divorce statistics have only recently begun to be accurately kept.
     c.   researchers have failed to focus enough attention on this area.
     d.   elderly research subjects are hesitant to talk about their marital
           relationships.

24. Divorce is most common during which age range?

    a.   18 - 30.
*   b.   30 - 45.
    c.   45 - 60.
    d.   60 and older.

25. Which of the following was mentioned in the text as a methodological problem associated with the study of sexuality and aging?

    a.   Older adults are known to lose the capacity to perform sexually.
    b.   It is difficult to recruit older subjects for studies concerned with sexuality.
    c.   Older adults tend to distort the frequency with which they engage in heterosexual behavior.
*   d.   It is difficult to operationally define heterosexual behavior.

26. Which of the following was <u>NOT</u> reported in the text as a significant conclusion of studies concerning male sexuality and aging?

    a.   As age increases, fewer men are sexually active.
    b.   Older males are less sexually active than younger men.
    c.   Older males lose the physical capacity to perform sexually.
    d.   Many males remain sexually active throughout adulthood.

27. According to Masters and Johnson, the most important factor in the maintenance of effective sexual behavior in aging males is

*   a.   consistency of active sexual expression.
    b.   the availability of an attractive partner.
    c.   the absence of latent homosexual tendencies.
    d.   that the male refrains from masturbation.

28. Compared to men of the same age, women tend to have sexual intercourse

*   a.   less frequently.
    b.   more frequently.
    c.   about the same amount.
    d.   rarely.

29. Which of these factors was <u>NOT</u> reported in the text as influencing sexual activity among older men?

    a.   Consistency of sexual expression throughout adulthood.
    b.   Physical health.
*   c.   Marital status.
    d.   Attitudes toward sexuality.

30. Women tend to reach their sexual peak during what age range?

    a.   Late teens.
    b.   Mid twenties.
*   c.   Mid thirties.
    d.   Women generally do not reach a sexual peak.

31. Which of the following conclusions was reported in the text concerning female sexuality and aging?

    a.   The sexual capacity of women declines markedly with increasing age.
*   b.   The sexual capacity of women declines little with increasing age.
    c.   The sexual activity of women declines little with increasing age.
    d.   Elderly women tend to become inorgasmic with increasing age.

32. One of the factors which seems to influence the sexual activity of older females is

    a.   socioeconomic status.
    b.   hormonal levels.
    c.   religious affiliation.
*   d.   marital status.

33. One of the difficulties associated with drawing conclusions about age-related homosexual behavior is that

*   a.   few empirical studies have been conducted on this topic.
    b.   most elderly homosexuals are in mental institutions.
    c.   homosexual behavior is difficult to define.
    d.   homosexual behavior is practically nonexistent among elderly adults.

34. One reason for the decline since 1900 in the number of elderly adults who reside with their adult children is that

    a.   society's attitudes toward the aged have worsened in the past fifty years.
    b.   the elderly have a shorter life span than they did in 1900.
    c.   most elderly adults are now placed in nursing homes.
*   d.   the financial status of the aged has drastically improved since 1900.

35. Providing care for an aging parent is likely to become easier in the future because

    a.   the government is instituting many new programs that will help caregivers.
    b.   the ratio of parents to children will decrease.
    c.   most chronic disabilities of late life will be remediated.
*   d.   none of the above.

36. Which of the following was <u>NOT</u> mentioned in the text as a difficulty facing adult children in the care of their elderly parents?

*   a.   Elderly parents often claim to be entitled to be cared for by their adult children.
    b.   Caring for an elderly parent can be financially stressful.
    c.   Caregivers are more vulnerable to depression and anger.
    d.   Elderly parents often resent losing their independence.

37. The percentage of older Americans with children who have grandchildren is approximately

    a.   one out of two.
    b.   three out of four.
*   c.   nine out of ten.
    d.   one out of five.

38. Which of the following was <u>NOT</u> identified by Neugarten and Weinstein's study as a specific style of behavior for grandparents?

    a.   Fun-seeker.
    b.   Surrogate parent.
*   c.   Valued elder.
    d.   Reservoir of family wisdom.

39. In Kivnick's (1982) study which was discussed in the text, grandparents who themselves had a favorite grandparent during childhood were more likely to perceive themselves as a

*   a.   Valued elder.
         b.   Spoiler and indulger.
         c.   Surrogate parent.
         d.   Fun-seeker.

40. The topics of conversation which are typically avoided by grandparents and grandchildren because of the controversial nature are referred to in the text as

         a.   safe subjects.
         b.   neutralized topics.
*   c.   demilitarized zones.
         d.   friendly chats.

41. One of the difficulties faced by social scientists in formulating standard styles of grandparenting is

*   a.   the wide range of ages for both grandparents and grandchildren.
         b.   present-day grandparents have increasingly less contact with their grandchildren than ever before.
         c.   most grandparents reside in nursing homes or other institutions.
         d.   grandchildren today tend to have negative stereotypes of grandparents.

42. According to one theory, the combination of age and gender are powerful determinants of people's social roles and their interpersonal behavior. This theory is referred to as

         a.   exchange theory.
         b.   activity theory.
         c.   disengagement theory.
*   d.   role theory.

43. Conceptually, Continuity theory is most closely linked to

*   a.   disengagement and activity theories.
         b.   exchange and role theories.
         c.   exchange theory only.
         d.   all of the above.

CHAPTER 9--WORK AND RETIREMENT

CHAPTER OBJECTIVES

The purpose of this chapter is to enable students to:

Identify and define key concepts related to work and retirement.

Identify factors that contribute to job satisfaction.

Differentiate between intrinsic and extrinsic factors.

Identify gender-related issues that impact on job satisfaction.

Describe the changing role of women in the work force.

Describe the relationship between job performance and aging; differentiate between myths/stereotypes and scientific evidence.

Identify factors which affect the decision to retire.

Identify and describe issues that affect satisfaction with retirement.

Describe how the social security system works and the economic future of the elderly.

Understand the difference between Medicare (Parts A and B) and Medicaid.

DISCUSSION QUESTIONS

Describe the meaning of work in your life; compare and contrast your view of work with that of your parents. What factors have shaped your view and your parents' views of work?

What impact(s) might the changing demographic trends in the U.S. have on the work force in this country over the next 50 years? How might these trends impact on your own work life?

What type of working life do you expect to have? When will your working life come to an end? What factors do you think will lead you to retire?

What are the likely tax consequences of a changing dependency ratio? How will future generations be able to support the young and elderly?

How would a universal health care program affect Medicare and Medicaid?

LEARNING ACTIVITIES

Interview several people who are at different stages in their careers (e.g., beginning, middle, close to retirement). Find out their level of job satisfaction and the factors that contribute to this level of satisfaction.

Interview a man and a woman who have comparable jobs. How do they see the relationship between their work and family? What are their reasons for working? What is their level of job satisfaction, and what factors contribute to their feelings of satisfaction/dissatisfaction? Compare and contrast the answers you receive from each. To what extent do you think gender has influenced their views of work?

Interview a person who has recently retired. Find out why s/he retired. What does being retired mean to the person? What effect has retirement had on this person's life style, and what adjustments has s/he had to make? Have these adjustments been easy or difficult?

Locate a business or organization that offers pre-retirement planning courses and find out: what is taught; who attends the courses; and how participants react to the course.

ADDITIONAL READINGS

Introductory

Rowe, J. W., & Kahn, R. L. 1998. Successful Aging. (New York: Pantheon).

Intermediate

Cleveland, J. N., & Shore, L. M. 1996. "Work and Employment." In J. E. Birren (Ed.). Encyclopedia of Gerontology, Vol. II (pp. 627-639). (New York: Academic Press).

Advanced

Schulz, J. H. 1995. "Economic Security Policies." In R. H. Binstock & L. K. George (Eds.), Handbook of Aging and the Social Sciences, 4th Ed. (pp. 410-426). (New York: Academic Press).

MULTIPLE CHOICE QUESTIONS

1. Since 1900 the proportion of the life span that is spent in labor force participation has increased most dramatically for

*   a.   women.
        b.   men.
        c.   children.
        d.   retired persons.

2. The extent to which work is gratifying and enjoyable for its own sake is known as

*   a.   intrinsic benefits of work.
        b.   extrinsic benefits of work.
        c.   job satisfaction.
        d.   occupational well-being.

3. Extrinsic aspects of work

        a.   are unrelated to its intrinsic aspects.
*   b.   refers to the influence of work on home and family life.
        c.   are more important than intrinsic aspects.
        d.   determine one's progression up the career ladder.

4. One reason for the equivocal results in studies of aging and work performance appears to be

*   a.   the limited information provided by chronological age.
        b.   the failure of these studies to take job satisfaction into account.
        c.   the differences between men and women in job performance.
        d.   the fact that the samples are limited by the mandatory retirement laws.

5. One of the goals of an industrial social psychologist would be

*   a.   to make the workplace more conducive to the needs and wants of its employees.
        b.   to assess workers of their managerial capabilities.
        c.   to weed out nonproductive employees.
        d.   to aid aging workers with retirement planning.

6. The extent to which one likes or dislikes various aspects of work, including the work itself, relationships with coworkers, working conditions, etc. is called

*   a.   job satisfaction.
       b.   occupational appraisal.
       c.   employee well-being.
       d.   job security.

7. Research on aging on aging and job satisfaction clearly shows that the relationship between age and job satsifaction is

       a.   U-shaped, initially high followed by a decline and then an increase
       b.   linear and positive.
       c.   linear and negative.
*   d.   none of the above.

8. According to the United States Department of Labor, an employee over the age of 55 is called

*   a.   an older worker.
       b.   a senior staff member.
       c.   a pre-retirement worker.
       d.   a high absenteeism risk.
       e.   a mature worker.

9. By 1993, the number of age discrimination complaints

*   a.   reached 15,000 per year.
       b.   began to decline significantly.
       c.   began in increase rapidly.
       d.   reached 1,000,000.

10. Which of the following was NOT mentioned in the text as a stereotype held by managers about older workers?

       a.   older workers are uncreative.
       b.   older workers are untrainable.
*   c.   older workers are lazy.
       d.   older workers are slow to make decisions.

11. According to the best available data midlife career changes are most often the result of

     a.   failing to realize one's potential.
     b.   finding a new career that is potentially more satisfying.
     c.   changing one's life goals due to external circumstances.
     d.   feelings of boredom and stagnation.
*   e.   none of the above

12. The term used to describe all people who are employed, plus those who are unemployed but looking for work is

*   a.   labor force.
     b.   vested workers.
     c.   job market.
     d.   employment statistics.

13. The percent of women who make up the labor force has increased dramatically in the last few decades. In 1996 they made up approximately what percent of the labor force?

*   a.   60%
     b.   90%
     c.   40%
     d.   32%

14. Although women have made significant gains in the types of jobs they hold, they are still not highly represented in occupations such as

     a.   accountants.
*   b.   mathematical and computer scientists.
     c.   managerial positions.
     d.   none of the above.

15. Which of the following was NOT mentioned in the text as a difficulty in the establishment of an effective comparable worth system?

     a.   women are more likely than men to interrupt their careers in order to raise children.
     b.   some women tend to choose low level jobs in exchange for flexibility.
     c.   it is difficult to evaluate the demands made by different jobs.
*   d.   sex discrimination has not been demonstrated to exist in the workplace.

16. Which of the following was <u>NOT</u> mentioned in the text as a factor likely to contribute to a women's inter-role conflict?

      a.   if the woman has young children.
*   b.   if the woman has higher levels of career aspiration.
      c.   if the woman's decision to work is not supported by her husband.
      d.   if the woman earns more money than her husband.

17. The proportion of individuals who work part time after retirement has

*   a.   increased in recent decades.
      b.   decreased in recent decades.
      c.   stayed about the same.
      d.   increased only for women.

18. Since 1900, the proportion of older people who retire

*   a.   has increased dramatically.
      b.   has increased slightly.
      c.   has decreased dramatically.
      d.   has remained about the same.

19. Leaving the work force prior to the age mandated by the employer or by law is a term called

*   a.   early retirement.
      b.   honeymoon period.
      c.   premature termination.
      d.   disenchantment phase.

20. One difficulty with the studies concluding a significant negative relationship between age and attitudes toward retirement is

*   a.   their vulnerability to cohort effects.
      b.   the fact that these studies polled only manual laborers.
      c.   their failure to account for gender differences.
      d.   their failure to take mandatory retirement laws into consideration.

21. The group most likely to opt for early retirement is

    a.   middle level employees.
    b.   higher level employees.
    c.   lower level employees.
    d.   the self-employed.

22. Most men who opt for early retirement under Social Security cite which of the following reasons for doing so?

    a.   health.
    b.   societal pressure.
    c.   job dissatisfaction.
    d.   family problems.

23. The first of the phases of retirement suggested by theorists such as Atchley is

    a.   the honeymoon phase.
    b.   the disenchantment phase.
    c.   the reorientation phase.
    d.   the termination phase.

24. The phase of retirement in which the individual adjusts to the realities of retirement and seeks out new activities is called

    a.   the reorientation phase.
    b.   the retirement routine phase.
    c.   the honeymoon phase.
    d.   the termination phase.

25. The most important inference to be drawn from the phase model of retirement is that

    a.   some individuals adjust to retirement better than others.
    b.   the phases of retirement are predictable and sequential.
    c.   it is better to retire voluntarily than to be mandated to retire.
    d.   the honeymoon phase of retirement is a myth.

26. One difficulty with the studies concluding adverse financial effects of retirement is that

*   a.   only cross-sectional data was included.
       b.   only lower level employees were studied.
       c.   only female workers were studied.
       d.   the studies failed to take pension benefits into account.

27. Longitudinal studies of the financial effects of retirement have suggested that an important predictive factor for financial difficulties is

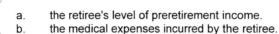

*   a.   the retiree's level of preretirement income.
       b.   the medical expenses incurred by the retiree.
       c.   the marital status of the retiree.
       d.   whether the retiree had invested in an Individual Retirement Account.

28. The most likely cause of deteriorating health after retirement appears to be

*   a.   deteriorating preretirement health.
       b.   poor medical programs for the elderly.
       c.   the stress associated with retirement.
       d.   increased arguments with spouses.

29. One factor that has been shown to be significant in predicting the effect of retirement on the marital relationship is

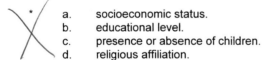

*   a.   socioeconomic status.
       b.   educational level.
       c.   presence or absence of children.
       d.   religious affiliation.

30. Poverty rates among persons over the age of 65 are highest for

       a.   widowed women.
       b.   blacks.
       c.   people whose sole source of income is social security.
*   d.   black women living alone.

31. The migration rates for individuals who reach retirement age

*   a.   rises slightly from preretirement levels.
        b.   rises dramatically from preretirement levels.
        c.   neither rises nor declines from preretirement levels.
        d.   declines slightly from preretirement levels.

32. In general, one of the effects of retirement seems to be

*   a.   a drop in income.
        b.   declines in health.
        c.   increased feeling of depression.
        d.   increased marital strife.

33. The dependency ratio refers to the

        a.   ratio of men to women.
        b.   children to adults.
*   c.   workers to non-workers.
        d.   disabled to able-bodied.

34. By the year 2030, it is expected that for every non-worker in our society there will be

        a.   two workers.
*   b.   one worker.
        c.   four workers.
        d.   three workers.

35. Income gains of the elderly during the last few decades are expected to

        a.   be lost in the future.
        b.   continue for another 4 decades.
        c.   come to a halt in the next two decades.
        d.   none of the above.

36. By the year 2022 you will have to be what age in order to receive full social security benefits?

        a.   64
        b.   65
*   c.   67
        d.   70

37. Medicare Part A pays for all of the following benefits except

      a.   inpatient hospital care.
      b.   skilled nursing facility care.
      c.   home health care.
      d.   hospice care.
*   e.   physician visits.

38. One of the major problems with Medicare is that

      a.   costs have escalated too quickly.
      b.   it doesn't cover all of the acute health care needs of the elderly.
      c.   it doesn't cover most of the long term care needs of the elderly.
*   d.   all of the above.

39. Medicaid is a combined federal and state program that pays for

*   a.   health care of the poor.
      b.   health care of the elderly poor.
      c.   health care of children.
      e.   health care of the disabled.

40. Paying for Social Security is unlikely to create problems until

      a.   the year 2001.
*   b.   the baby boomers begin to retire.
      c.   the year 2050.
      f.   none of the above.

CHAPTER 10--STRESS AND COPING

CHAPTER OBJECTIVES

The purpose of this chapter is to enable students to:

Identify and define key concepts related to stress and coping.

Compare and contrast alternative definitions of stress; identify the contributions and limitations of each.

Differentiate among three stress research traditions—environmental, psychological, and biological traditions.

Identify the components of a general model of stress and explain how they are interrelated.

Apply the general model of stress to family caregiving as an example.

Describe the relationship between aging, stress and coping ability.

Describe how stress might affect illness and mortality.

DISCUSSION QUESTIONS

What are major life stressors throughout adult life course likely to be? Have members of your immediate or extended family experienced any of these stressors? If so, what has been the impact on the family?

Is stress positive or negative? Defend your position.

Using the "The Social Readjustment Rating Scale" on page 283, identify the number of stressful life events you have experienced during the past two years. According to this rating scale, is your life high or low in stress? Does this match with your own perception of the degree of stress in your life? Why or why not?

When you experience stress, what coping strategies do you use?

LEARNING ACTIVITIES

Ask 10 people you know to rate the amount of stress in their lives during the past two years using the Social Readjustment Rating Scale on page 283. Try to obtain responses from adults of different ages and record each person's age on the rating sheet. After the person completes the scale, ask how they coped with stressful events. Bring the information you gather to class. Compare your information with that gathered by your classmates. Group the responses by age and see if there are major differences either in the occurrence of stressful events or in coping strategies for different age groups. Explain how the information gathered by your class either supports or contradicts what is known about the relationship between aging, stress and coping.

ADDITIONAL READINGS

Introductory

Schulz, R., O'Brien, A, T., Bookwala, J., & Fleissner, K. 1995. "Psychiatric and Physical Morbidity Effects of Alzheimer's Disease Caregiving: Prevalence, Correlates, and Causes." The Gerontologist: 35, 771-791.

Intermediate

McLeod, J. D. 1996. "Life Events." In J. E. Birren (Ed.) Encyclopedia of Gerontology, Vol. II (pp. 41-51). (New York: Academic Press).

Advanced

Cohen, S., Kessler, R. C., & Gordon, L. U. 1995. "Strategies for Measuring Stress in Studies of Psychiatric and Physical Disorders." In S. Cohen & L. U. Gordon (Eds.), Measuring Stress (pp. 3-26). (New York: Oxford University Press).

MULTIPLE CHOICE QUESTIONS

1. All of the following are examples of stressors except

    a.   boredom and understimulation.
    b.   conflicts.
    c.   frustration.
    d.   disappointments.
    e.   daily hassles.
*   f.   rewards.

2. The type of stressors that have a cumulative effect when occurring in quick succession of one another are called

*   a.   a martyrdom of pinpricks.
    b.   noxious stimuli.
    c.   external pressures and overstimulation.
    d.   conflicts.

3. The tendency to resolve a stressful situation by either attacking or escaping is referred to as the

*   a.   fight or flight reaction.
    b.   emotion-focused coping.
    c.   problem-focused coping.
    d.   general adaptation syndrome.

4. Hans Selye's proposed pattern of responses to a stressful situation, which consists of three stages is called

*   a.   the General Adaptation Syndrome.
    b.   the Fight or Flight Reaction.
    c.   the Alarm Reaction.
    d.   the Defense Mechanism Syndrome.

5. The first stage of the General Adaptation Syndrome, which describes the body's initial responses to a stressful situation is called

*   a.   the alarm reaction.
    b.   the stage of resistance.
    c.   the stage of exhaustion.
    d.   the fight or flight reaction.

6. The stage in the General Adaptation Syndrome in which the body tries to limit the effects of the stressful situation is called

*   a.   the stage of resistance.
     b.   the stage of exhaustion.
     c.   the defense mechanism phase.
     d.   the alarm reaction.

7. According to Selye, the experience of stress is always accompanied by

*   a.   physiological changes.
     b.   feelings of helplessness.
     c.   adaptive coping strategies.
     d.   behavioral changes.

8. Among modern stress researchers, individuals who focus on events that are normatively thought to be adapative challenges would fall into the

*   a.   environmental tradition.
     b.   biological tradition.
     c.   psychological tradition.
     d.   all of the above.

9. The psychological stress research approach places strong emphasis on
*   a.   the individual's evaluation of the potential harm posed by environmental event.
     b.   the individual's physiological response to a psychological event.
     c.   the subjective nature of all coping responses to a threat.
     d.   all of the above.

10. The biological stress research tradition

     a.   is most closely linked to the work of Cannon and Selye.
     b.   focuses on the activation of specific physiological systems.
     c.   emphasizes physical and psychiatric disorders as outcomes.
*   d.   all of the above.

11. In evaluating the three modern stress research traditions, the best general conclusion is that

    a.   the psychological tradition has the greatest amount of empirical support.
    b.   they complement each other.
    c.   the environmental tradition is losing favor because of the lack of clear findings.
    d.   all of the above.

12. One goal of the general stress-health process model is to

    a.   show how the three stress research traditions can be integrated.
    b.   explain how stress can result in illness.
    c.   demonstrate the role of emotions.
    d.   all of the above.

13. When applied to family caregiving, the stress-health process model shows

    a.   why perceived burden is the primary outcome of most caregiving studies.
    b.   how some caregivers might become depressed.
    c.   why many caregivers find the experience positive.
    d.   none of the above.

14. Which of the following was NOT listed in the text as a methodological criticism of Holmes and Rahe's Social Readjustment Rating Scale?

    a.   The scale implies that stressful events cause physical illnesses.
    b.   The scale focuses on those events that require significant readjustments in living.
    c.   The scale contains many items that are more likely to happen to young adults.
    d.   The scale contains many items that are too complicated to easily understand.

15. One solution that has been proposed in response to the methodological criticisms of Holmes and Rahe's Social Readjustment Scale is to

     *   a.   collapse the various life events into major categories.
           b.   develop chronological age norms.
           c.   limit the use of the scale to young adults only.
           d.   increase the number of items dealing with major life readjustments.

16. Research conducted by Richard Lazarus has suggested that the stressor which predicts psychosomatic illnesses significantly better than life events is

           a.   daily hassles.
           b.   socioeconomic pressures.
           c.   poor nutritional habits.
           d.   marital conflict.

17. One problem with the conclusions drawn from research studies that investigated the effect of relocation on mortality rates among the elderly is that

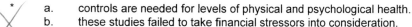

     *   a.   controls are needed for levels of physical and psychological health.
           b.   these studies failed to take financial stressors into consideration.
           c.   the studies relied solely on cross-sectional data.
           d.   no allowance was made for effects of relocation distance.

18. Among the elderly, research has suggested that the effects of divorce

     *   a.   are more stressful than the effects of widowhood.
           b.   are less stressful than the effects of widowhood.
           c.   are about as stressful as the effects of widowhood.
           d.   depend largely on financial status of the couple.

19. The behavioral style that is characterized by ambition, competitiveness, aggressiveness, and perfectionism has been called

     *   a.   Type A behavior.
           b.   Type B behavior.
           c.   aggressive personality disorder.
           d.   obsessive-compulsive disorder.

20. Recent research suggests that the negative health effects attributable to being Type A is probably better explained by

    a.   the timidity of Type As.
    b.   the anger and hostility of Type As.
    c.   the time urgency of Type As.
    d.   all of the above.

21. For normal elderly adults, the research evidence indicates that the ability to cope with stressful normative life events

    a.   increases.
    b.   decreases.
    c.   remains the same.
    d.   is impossible to measure.

22. Dealing with stress by taking action intended to resolve or change the existing situation is called

    a.   problem-focused coping.
    b.   emotion-focused coping.
    c.   defense mechanisms.
    d.   fight or flight coping.

23. Dealing with stress by trying to achieve acceptance of the existing situation is called

    a.   problem-focused coping.
    b.   emotion-focused coping.
    c.   defense mechanisms.
    d.   fight or flight responses.

24. An example of emotion-focused coping would best be typified by which of the following statements?

    a.   "I looked for the silver lining."
    b.   "I got the person responsible to change his mind."
    c.   "I made a plan of action and followed it."
    d.   "I stood my ground and fought for what I wanted."

25. An example of problem-focused coping would best typified by which of the following statements?

a. "I got the person responsible to change his mind."
b. "I accepted sympathy and understanding from another person."
c. "I tried to forget the whole thing."
e. "Even if I am bad off, there are many whose health is worse."

26. Emotion-focused coping may be more adaptive for the elderly than problem-focused coping because

a. the elderly have reduced cognitive capacity.
b. the elderly are less active.
c. the types of problems encountered are less controllable.
d. all of the above.

90

CHAPTER 11--ADULT PSYCHOPATHOLOGY

CHAPTER OBJECTIVES

The purpose of this chapter is to enable students to:

Identify and define key concepts related to psychopathology and aging.

Differentiate the myths from scientific evidence regarding psychopathology and aging.

Identify the major risk factors for various psychiatric conditions.

Explain the purpose of DSM-IV.

Identify methods for diagnosis and assessment of psychopathology.

Identify and describe guidelines that increase the effectiveness of a clinical interview when assessing an older adult.

Contrast the incidence and prevalence of major categories of psychopathology among the 65+ age group, and explain the extent to which each disease is related to the aging process.

Describe criteria used to diagnose dementia, depression and anxiety disorders.

Describe the use of major categories of treatment procedures, and compare and contrast the advantages/disadvantages of each.

DISCUSSION QUESTIONS

View the first two segments of the videotape, My Mother, My Father, and discuss the ways in which your family's lifestyle would be affected by a relative afflicted by Alzheimer's Disease.

Choose one category of psychopathology discussed in this chapter and find out the incidence and prevalence of this disease in your hometown or the city/town where you are attending college.

Use a book such as Assessing the Elderly by Kane and Kane to examine various instruments used to assess depression, cognitive functioning, and other mental health problems of the elderly. Present to your class a description of the instrument, its purpose, and its strengths and weaknesses as an assessment tool. Compare and contrast the instrument you examine with those examined by your classmates.

LEARNING ACTIVITIES

Find out whether there is a medical or mental health facility in your hometown or the city/town where you are attending college that specializes in the assessment and treatment of psychopathology among the elderly. Arrange for a tour of the facility, and talk with staff to learn what assessment and treatment procedures are used at the facility.

Visit a day care center for patients suffering from Alzheimer's Disease and talk with staff to learn what are the needs of these individuals and what procedures are used to meet these needs.

Visit an alcohol evaluation and treatment center or an Alcoholics Anonymous group. Talk with staff/members about the problems of alcohol and drug abuse throughout the adult years. Learn how these problems are treated.

ADDITIONAL READINGS

Introductory

Koenig, H. G. 1995. Research on Religion and Aging. (Westport, CT: Greenwood Press).

Intermediate

Reynolds III, C. F., Zubenko, G. S, Pollock, B. G., Mulsant, B. H., Schulz, R., Mintun, M. A., Mazumdar, & Kupfer, D. J. 1994. "Depression in Late Life." Current Opinion in Psychiatry: 7, 18-21.

Advanced

Penninx, B, Guralnick, J. M., Mendes de Leon, C. G., et al. 1998. "Cardiovascular Events and Morality in Newly and Chronically Depressed Persons > 70 Years of Age." American Journal of Cardiology: 81, 988-994.

MULTIPLE CHOICE QUESTIONS

1. Whether or not a particular behavior is considered pathological may depend on

    a.   the culture of the individual.
    b.   his or her age.
    c.   the context in which it occurs.
*   d.   all of the above.

2. The DSM-IV is a classification system for

*   a.   mental disorders.
    b.   approaches to psychotherapy.
    c.   assessment procedures.
    d.   antidepressants.

3. Modern clinicians agree that all of the following could be causes of psychopathology except

    a.   childhood experiences.
    b.   biological factors such as endocrine disorders, infections or dietary deficiencies.
*   c.   religious participation.
    d.   exposure to severe stressors.

4. Being elderly and socially integrated have been found to be

*   a.   protective of mental health.
    b.   positively associated with psychopathology.
    c.   not associated with mental health.
    d.   none of the above.

5. All of the following are essential components of a good psychiatric interview with geriatric patients except

    a.   history.
    b.   physical examination.
    c.   mental status examination.
*   d.   projective test.

6. Which of the following was <u>NOT</u> mentioned in the text as a characteristic of an effective clinical interview with an elderly patient?

a.   Tests of intellectual capacity are scattered throughout the interview.
b.   The patient is allowed to talk spontaneously about his or her problems at the opening and close of the interview.
c.   The interview's length is limited to the patient's attention span.
*   d.   Distressing or emotionally laden topics should be avoided.

7. Psychometric instruments can be useful diagnostic tools because they

*   a.   take only a few minutes to administer.
b.   provide accurate clinical diagnoses.
c.   are culturally sensitive.
d.   all of the above.

8. The study of the distribution of illnesses in time and place, and of the factors which influence this distribution is known as

*   a.   epidemiology.
b.   psychopathology.
c.   biostatistics.
d.   prevalence rate.

9. Determining how often various forms of psychopathology occurs by the examination of hospital or therapist records is called

*   a.   the case register method.
b.   the field survey method.
c.   the prevalence rate survey.
d.   the incidence rate survey.

10. The number of new cases of a particular disorder that occur during a specified period is called the

a.   incidence rate.
b.   prevalence rate.
c.   case register rate.
d.   population at risk.

11. A term used to describe all people of a specified geographic area who could conceivably contract the disorder under study is called

*   a.   population at risk.
      b.   prevalence rate.
      c.   incidence rate.
      d.   case register sample.

12. The total number of people in a given community who suffer from a disorder under investigation would be called the

*   a.   prevalence rate.
      b.   incidence rate.
      c.   disorder density.
      d.   population at risk.

13. Symptoms of dementia include

      a.   decline in intellectual ability.
      b.   impairments in memory, judgment, and abstract thinking.
      c.   language problems.
      d.   failure to recognize familiar objects.
      e.   three of the above.
*   f.   all of the above.

14. According to recent studies, the percent of people age 85 and over with probable Alzheimer's disease is

      a.   12%
*   b.   20%
      c.   47%
      d.   61%

15. All of the following have been identified as possible causes or correlates of Alzheimer's disease except the following

      a.   genetics.
      b.   high amounts of trace metals in the brain.
      c.   malfunctioning cholinergic system.
*   d.   high levels of lifetime alcohol consumption.
      e.   serotonergic system dysfuntion.

16. The course of Alzheimer's disease would most accurately be described as a

*   a.   steady deterioration.
        b.   sudden onset followed by quick recovery.
        c.   rapid decline.
        d.   stepwise decline.

17. The cause of Vascular dementia is thought to be the result of

        a.   genetic determinants.
        b.   viral influences.
*   c.   inadequate blood supply to the brain.
        d.   the presence of trace metals in the brain.

18. Which of the following was <u>NOT</u> mentioned in the text as a symptom of clinical depression?

        a.   Hopelessness about the future.
        b.   Somatic complaints.
*   c.   Intermittent periods of euphoria.
        d.   Distorted perceptions and thoughts.

19. Among elderly patients, depression is often misdiagnosed as

*   a.   dementia
        b.   schizophrenia.
        c.   advanced alcoholism.
        d.   neurosis.

20. One way to differentiate organically caused dementia from depression-related dementia is

*   a.   by the reversibility of depression-related dementia.
        b.   through a Mental Status Examination.
        c.   through the administration of intelligence tests.
        d.   the relative response to electroconvulsive therapy.

21. The relationship between physical illness and depression appears to be influenced by

*   a.   the degree of physical impairment associated with the illness.
        b.   the gender of the patient.
        c.   the side effects of medication.
        d.   the quality of medical care.

22. The prevalence of major depression among the elderly is thought to be

*   a.   less than 5%
         b.   6 to 10%
         c.   about 15%
         d.   about 30%

23. All of the following are popular treatments of depression except

         a.   electroconvulsive therapy.
*   b.   psychosurgery.
         c.   drug therapy
         d.   cognitive therapy
         e.   behavior therapy

24. All of the following are examples of anxiety disorders except

         a.   generalized anxiety.
         b.   phobic disorders.
         c.   obsessive compulsive disorders.
*   d.   neurosis.

25. Like other forms of psychopathology, the incidence of anxiety disorders tends to

         a.   increase with age.
*   b.   decrease with age.
         c.   stay the same with age.
         d.   decrease only among men.

26. Treatment(s) of choice for anxiety disorders include

         a.   behavior therapy.
         b.   psychotherapy.
         c.   drug therapy such as benzodiazepines.
*   d.   all of the above.

CHAPTER 12--DEATH AND DYING

CHAPTER OBJECTIVES

The purpose of this chapter is to enable students to:

Identify and define key concepts relevant to death and dying.

Describe important demographic changes that have occurred since 1900 in the causes and places of death; identify the factors that have contributed to these changes.

Describe and understand differences in causes of death as a function of gender and race.

Describe the methodological difficulties associated with the study of death anxiety.

Compare and contrast the scientific evidence on death anxiety as an importance aspect of the human experience.

Describe the impact of terminal illness on health care professionals and compare and contrast the effectiveness of various coping strategies used by these professionals.

Describe the five stages of dying as proposed by Kubler-Ross and summarize the scientific evidence regarding the validity of this concept.

Describe the physical and socioemotional needs of the terminally ill.

Contrast the process of normal versus pathological grieving.

Explain the impact of the death of a spouse on the mortality rate of the survivor; include risk factors that affect mortality.

Describe therapeutic interventions in the grieving process.

DISCUSSION QUESTIONS

What do you think are some of the differences between dying at middle and old age?

What do you think are some of the differences between expected versus unexpected death?

Give examples of the fear of death as a destructive force; as a creative force.

LEARNING ACTIVITIES

Visit a hospice and identify the ways in which the physical and socioemotional needs of the patients and their families are met. Give a class report on this experience and your reactions to it.

Plan and conduct a debate on the issue of euthanasia and/or the right to die.

Plan and conduct a debate on the issue, "Should a patient with a terminal illness be informed of his/her condition?"

Recently, increased attention has been given to the concept of a "living will." Closely examine the living will form in the text book. What are some of the pros and cons of completing such a form? Under what circumstances would you want to have a living will for yourself, and have it followed?

ADDITIONAL READINGS

Introductory

Prigerson, H. G., Shear, M. K., Bierhals, A. J., et al. 1997. "Case Histories of Traumatic Grief." Omega: Journal of Death and Dying: 35, 9-24.

Intermediate

Van Der Kloot Meijburg, H. H. 1995-96. "How Health Care Institutions in the Netherlands Approach Physciain Assisted Death. Omega Journal of Death and Dying: 32, 179-196.

Moss, M. S., Resch, N., & Moss, S. Z. 1997. "The Role of Gender in Middle-Age Chirdren's Responses to Parent Death. Omega: Journal of Death and Dying: 35, 43-65.

Advanced

Prigerson, H. G., Bierhals, A. J., Kasl, S. V., Reynolds, C. F., Shear, M. K., Day, N., Beery, L C., Newsom, J. T., & Jacobs, S. 1997. "Traumatic Grief as a Risk Factor for Mental and Physical Morbidity. American Journal of Psychiatry: 154, 616-623.

MULTIPLE CHOICE QUESTIONS

1. Deaths from each of the following causes have declined in the last few decades except

    a.   stroke.
    b.   heart disease.
    c.   Accidents.
    d.   acquired immunodeficiency syndrome (AIDS).
*   e.   none of the above, they have all declined.

2. According to the text, in 1998, the number one cause of death for both men and women was

    a.   cancer.
*   b.   heart disease.
    c.   suicide.
    d.   accidents.

3. The suicide rates for which of the following groups increases dramatically as a function of age

    a.   white females.
*   b.   white males.
    c.   nonwhite females.
    d.   all groups.

4. Compared to 40 years ago you are more likely to die

    a..   at home than a hospital.
    b.   in a nursing home than in a hospital.
    c.   in a hospice than in a hospital.
*   d.   none of the above.

5. According to recent data, men are more likely than women to

    a.   die in a nursing home.
    b.   die in a hospice.
*   c.   die in a general hospital.
    d.   all of the above.

6. The branch of psychology that views death anxiety as a chief motivator of human behavior is known as

*   a.   existential psychology.
       b.   thanatological psychology.
       c.   physiological psychology.
       d.   gerontological psychology.

7. A written measure of death anxiety that taps the conscious and public levels is called

*   a.   a direct measure.
       b.   an indirect measure.
       c.   an external measure.
       d.   an obtrusive measure.

8. One advantage of direct measures of death anxiety is

*   a.   they have been found to be externally valid.
       b.   the scale cannot be falsified.
       c.   unconscious feelings can be easily measured.
       d.   they are immune to the halo effect.

9. One criticism that has been leveled against death anxiety research is that

*   a.   the concept is treated as unidimensional.
       b.   the concept is presumed to be too complex to be measured.
       c.   the studies have failed to include dying individuals.
       d.   the measures are vulnerable to cohort effects.

10. The relationship between aging and the fear of death appears to be moderated by

*   a.   physical health.
       b.   belief in the supernatural.
       c.   marital status.
       d.   risk-taking behaviors.

11. According to the text, physicians and nurses are most likely to cope with death and dying

*   a.   by employing defense mechanisms.
      b.   by undergoing psychotherapy.
      c.   by joining a support group.
      d.   by leaving the profession.

12. The first of the stage of dying that were outlined by Kubler-Ross and discussed in the text is

*   a.   denial.
      b.   anger.
      c.   depression.
      d.   bargaining.

13. The stage of dying that is characterized by the attempt to strike an agreement to postpone death is

*   a.   bargaining.
      b.   anger.
      c.   denial.
      d.   depression.

14. Which of the following was mentioned in the text as a criticism of Kubler-Ross' stages of dying theory?

*   a.   Her conclusions were based on subjective clinical observation.
      b.   Research has failed to support the existence of the denial stage.
      c.   Kubler-Ross was found to have fabricated her data.
      d.   The stages are vulnerable to cohort effects.

15. According to the text, for most patients the single most important need of terminal patients is

*   a.   the alleviation of physical pain.
      b.   the preservation of dignity.
      c.   the writing of a will.
      d.   the need for economic assistance.

16. Research has demonstrated that one way to aid terminal patients in the preservation of dignity and self-worth is to

*   a.   allow them to help plan their own treatment.
        b.   teach them about the five stages of death.
        c.   keep from them the terminal nature of their illness.
        d.   encourage them to seek psychotherapy.

17. The primary goal of the hospice approach is to

*   a.   help terminally ill patients continue their lives in the home environment.
        b.   educate hospital personnel about the special needs of the terminally ill.
        c.   lobby for the passage of euthanasia laws.
        d.   conduct research on the existence of an afterlife.

18. According to the National Hospice Study, which was discussed in the text, all of the following were mentioned as a source of strength to the terminal patient <u>except</u>

        a.   supportive friends.
        b.   religion.
        c.   being needed by someone else.
*   d.   the knowledge of having lived a full life.

19. Negative health effects after bereavement are more likely to be found when

*   a.   the bereaved person is young.
        b.   the bereaved person has social support.
        c.   the bereaved person is a woman.
        d.   all of the above.

20. Research which compared suddenly bereaved spouses with those having more time to anticipate their spouses death reported that

        a.   the suddenly bereaved group had much less difficulty coping with their loss.
        b.   the suddenly bereaved group had a much briefer bereavement period.
*   c.   the two groups did not differ in their response to death.
        d.   the group who had anticipated the loss had a higher suicide rate.

21. Normal grief differs from pathological grief in terms of

*   a.   duration and intensity.
     b.   the absence of anger.
     c.   the presence of crying.
     d.   the belief in God's will.

22. Which of the following is <u>NOT</u> a phase of normal bereavement?

     a.   Confusion, shock, and denial.
     b.   All-encompassing sorrow.
     c.   Recovery.
*   d.   Euphoria.

23. The long term prognosis for persons suffering from pathological grief

*   a.   tends to be unfavorable.
     b.   tends to be favorable.
     c.   is impossible to predict.
     d.   depends on whether the death is anticipated or unanticipated.

24. Persons suffering from a syndrome of having intrusive thoughts, distressing preoccupation with the deceased person, feeling futile, experiencing numbness, and detachment, are thought to have a condition called

     a.   late grief response.
     b.   early grief response.
     c.   normal grief response.
*   d.   traumatic grief response.

25. Which of the following is <u>NOT</u> a factor in identifying a high-risk individual who is unusually likely to suffer health problems following the death of a spouse?

     a.   The spouse's death was unexpected.
     b.   They have strong, persistent feelings of anger and guilt.
     c.   Their socioeconomic status is low.
*   d.   They tend to be more affiliated with religious organizations and activities.

26. What percentage of the bereaved have been estimated to be unable to resolve their grief by themselves?

     a.   10%.
*   b.   25%.
     c.   50%.
     d.   85%.

27. Grieving individuals who tend to be most in need of professional therapy tend to be

*   a.   those who behave in a stoic manner.
     b.   those who become overly emotionally expressive.
     c.   those who become angry and resentful.
     d.   those who do not experience the illusion that the dead loved one is present.

28. Overall, paraprofessional therapy and self-help groups for grieving individuals have been found by researchers to be

*   a.   effective in many situations.
     b.   ineffective except for pathological grief.
     c.   effective only for young children.
     d.   not as effective as professional therapy.

ISBN 0-13-082733-9

9 780130 827333

99991